KT-453-565

F. R. BARRY

To Recover Confidence

SCM PRESS LTD

334 01667 3

First published 1974
by SCM Press Ltd
56 Bloomsbury Street London

© SCM Press Ltd 1974

Printed in Great Britain by
Cox & Wyman Ltd
London, Fakenham and Reading

To Recover Confidence

Contents

Introductory Note   vii

1 Are we losing our nerve?   1

2 Who is God and who is man?   12

3 The question of truth   30
   Relativity with everything?
   Faith and reason
   Is it true?

4 Freedom and permissiveness   63
   Freedom
   Metaphysical freedom
   What is morality?
   Absolutes and relatives
   Morality and religion
   Christian morals and 'new moralities'

5 Otherworldliness and secularity   105
   Worldliness and godliness
   Why the church?

Index of Names   117

Introductory Note

A long time ago, in 1937 (the year of King George VI's coronation), the SCM Press, then under Hugh Martin – that widely loved ecumenical figure – asked me to write the first volume for the Religious Book Club. It was called *What has Christianity to Say?* I could write with a smashing drive when I was young, and that book made a certain impression at the time. Perhaps it did something of what it set out to do. It was meant to help Christians to recover confidence and to be able to stand fast in the evil day, at a very difficult and dangerous moment when men's hearts were failing them for fear as the clouds banked up for the Second World War. Amid the clash of rival ideologies claiming dominion over the human soul, it tried to assure them that our faith holds within it the secret of justice, freedom and hope for man. But it spoke to, and out of, a given situation. Many of those for whom I am now asked to write had not even been born when that book was published and could hardly imagine the world out of which it came. Nor could we, at that time, possibly have foreseen the situation in which we are today. As I said myself in the preface to it, that book 'inevitably and intentionally dates'.

What is at stake is still the human soul. But the dangers that threaten it now take different form and the problems that we have now to face are different problems. The world in which my generation grew up is in dissolution; only the old remember it. To us then, it seemed that the clear and obvious duty was to save England and the world from the mental and moral tyranny of Nazism, to make the world safe, if we could and dared, for freedom and to keep open at least the possibility of a Christian civilization in the West. Many lived, and died, nobly for that cause. Few of the new generation are aware of the price that was paid for the freedom they take for granted. More than that, there are many who deny that 'our' civilization was worth saving, though they have little idea what they want to put in its place, beyond being sure that it must be revolutionary. In the midst of the radical post-war revolution – social, technical, moral and intellectual – few of the older waymarks seem trustworthy, and none of the older securities secure. In 1937 we could still take Christian belief more or less for granted. No one had suggested that teaching it in schools was a wicked indoctrination by the establishment, or that the existence of God was a marginal question, if not already ruled out.[1] Today statements about the Christian faith are met with a blank incomprehension. The atmospheric pressures today are such that for most of us it is a great deal harder to believe in God than it was thirty years ago, and I feel those pressures as keenly as anyone else. Moreover, in our present confusion Christians themselves are shaken and uncertain. People today are asking different questions, and they do not see how traditional Christianity can be so understood or presented as to meet them. Attempts at theological restatement – rightly and bravely though they have been attempted – have seemed to be undermining the foundations and have left them still more confused and insecure. Is this still the light which can guide their steps through the fogs and frustrations of the world today? What has Christianity to say now, in this totally changed and daunting situation? Is it still viable? Can we still believe it?

That is what this book is intended to be about. Ostensibly, it was intended as a sequel – another treatment of the same subject by the same author nearly forty years later. But so much has happened in those forty years that it cannot be quite the same sort of book as its predecessor. For one thing, I am now myself an old man, and old men tend to look at things rather differently. The older a man gets, the more he realizes how mysterious are human life and death. However confident he may still be in his fundamental Christian beliefs, he will probably be less ready to dogmatize. In a sense, indeed, old men know too much. They will want to be putting in qualifying clauses, and their sentences will sound less like hammer-blows. And a man will have learnt, or certainly ought to have learnt, a great deal in the course of forty years; on some points his mind may have changed – if it hasn't, there must be something wrong with it. I have passed through a good many harrowing experiences, in the public world and in my private life, and have been forced to reflect fairly deeply about the tragic dimension in human life and, to that extent, to rethink my theology. I suspect that all the seven ages of man have their own particular form of religious experience, their own way of apprehending Christianity, and their own corresponding way of articulating it – i.e. their own kind of theological thinking. It may be in the end that the only gift which the old have the right or the capacity to offer to younger fellow-Christians setting out on their journey is experience – to warn them of dangerous short cuts, or of roads that have been found to end in precipices.

Moreover, since I first started to teach and write, the whole theological map has been redrawn or set out on a different projection. For one thing, the critical philosophy has made us more alive than some of our predecessors to the limitations of human knowledge. Theology in the past may have claimed to know more than we do know or ever can know. As William Temple taught us when he was growing old, we may have to begin again from what we do know.[2] I have been obliged, in my seventies and eighties, to revise quite a bit of my theological thinking. In the course of this. I have had to do my best to understand the new movements in philosophy which have seemed to many to deal fatal blows at the Christian faith or at any belief in God. Similarly, in the sphere of Christian conduct, I have done some fairly wide reading on ethical matters. As a result, I have come to see that the Christian faith cannot be defended just by repeated assertion, or Christian morals just by denunciation. Most of the objections against Christianity seem to rest either on misunderstanding or on plausible but fallacious arguments, which treat the passing fashions of thought, in a culture which is in process of transition, as though they were irrefragable statements of truth, with which Christian beliefs are incompatible. Rightly or wrongly, therefore, it has seemed to me that one way of helping perplexed Christians to recover confidence in their own position is to explore and exhibit the inadequacy of some of the widely accepted assumptions which are now being marketed as substitutes, and to show that the Christian faith makes better sense of the world and the life of man within it than some of the 'modern', sceptical alternatives.

So this is not such a forthright book as the other was. It leads readers by what may seem to some of them to be roundabout and rather remote tracks. The two longer argumentative chapters, on the question of truth and on freedom and permissiveness, are meant not to supply 'Christian answers' – I have lived to suspect ready-made Christian answers – but rather to offer the reader materials for thinking his own way through the confusions and cross-currents to which we are all exposed, and to be better equipped to defend the Christian case, arguing not from weakness but from strength. He alone can decide how far they succeed in that.

So the reader now knows what he is in for, and whether to start here or to throw down the book.

NOTES

1. But to take for granted a secularist world-view is not indoctrination; it is 'adult', progressive and democratic.

2. Cf. Howard Root, 'Beginning All Over Again', in A. R. Vidler (ed.), *Soundings*, Cambridge University Press, 1963, pp. 1–20.

1 | Are we losing our nerve?

At the end of his television lectures, Lord Clark, in his quiet, unemotional voice, gave a warning to us who inherited those cultural and spiritual achievements which he had so superbly represented. What kills a civilization, he said, more quickly than anything else, is lack of confidence. 'We can destroy ourselves by cynicism and disillusion, just as effectively as by bombs.'[1] Civilizations have perished before now through war, plague or natural catastrophes. They can also be destroyed from within. We can bring the whole human experiment to an end not only by a man-made nuclear holocaust but – as we are now being forcibly reminded – by our peacetime assaults on man's environment through pollution, waste and disturbance of the ecosphere.

These assaults have mental and spiritual grounds. Without some degree of material security there can be no civilization at all – only a 'war of everyman against everyman', in which life is nasty, brutish and short. But here, as always, there is a two-way traffic between mental and physical conditions. Doubts and spiritual insecurities can undermine the material foundations or disrupt the structural framework of a culture. Loss of confidence in a currency can lead to such uncontrollable inflation as to bring a whole society down in ruins. Loss of confidence in politicians can make a state virtually ungovernable, so that it sinks into anarchy and chaos.

Conversely, recovery of confidence, under new and inspiring leadership, for example, can lead to a national *risorgimento*, economic, political and moral. Confidence is one aspect of

1

faith. Loss of confidence is loss of faith – in life, in the world, in God and in man. It is that kind of cosmic disenchantment which threatens to bring our civilization down. Today cynicism and disillusion seem to be endemic in the air we breathe, not least in progressive and intellectual circles. There are ominous writings on the wall, suggesting that our society is passing into such an 'age of anxiety'[2] as that into which Christianity first came when the ancient culture began to sink in on itself amid the decline and fall of that Roman empire which had been commonly taken to be 'eternal'.

Anxiety is the fruit of insecurity – social and economic insecurity, and still more of insecurity in the cosmos – in face of the *finis* written by death. But it is a condition against which Jesus warns us, not – as in the *Angst* of the existentialists – a state of mind to be coveted or cultivated as one of the hallmarks of authentic living. In the moral theology of the church it has been reckoned a mortal sin (*accidie*). For it is the antithesis of trust in God and, as such, one of the roots of sin – introverted self-concern and self-centredness, separating man from God and neighbour.

When a social order begins to break down and men no longer have an established place in it and no longer feel that they belong, their sense of security is undermined and they tend to pass through a crisis of identity. 'Who am I?' they ask, 'and what am I here for anyway?' People do not ask that in a society which provides a stable and secure environment in which all have their recognized place and function, in which, moreover, all worship the same gods and acknowledge the same system of values. The *mores* of a traditional society seem to be so much part of the nature of things that they are invested with cosmic sanctions and ascribed to the ordinance of a divine lawgiver – as the commandments were handed down on Sinai. People may break the rules, but nobody questions them. When, however, under the impact of new forces, the old, coherent community life breaks down, there will be a corresponding religious crisis – a radical questioning, and perhaps rejection, of ancestral faiths and 'conventional' moralities; so that now, on top of their social insecurity, men are exposed to the ultimate insecurity of feeling themselves homeless and un-supported in a world that no longer validates their existence. Something of this kind seems to be happening now, as it has happened again and again before now – it is one of the com-monplaces of history. There is often, too, a disabling sense of guilt – such as can be traced in the Hellenistic Age, in Europe at the time of the Reformation, when men felt so urgent a need to be 'justified', and in contemporary post-war England with its feverish quest for status symbols and the preservation of differentials as the only way known for retaining self-re-spect.

In the second and third centuries after Christ this sense of spiritual insecurity was eating the heart out of the ancient culture; that was what made it an age of anxiety. Men lost confidence in themselves and in the social order which they inherited. The pagan gods had long since ceased to count. There was no divinity – nothing transcendent or meaningful – to be found here below. There was nothing left but a spiritual vacuum. The government, undermined by this loss of confidence, withdrew the legions from the frontiers to defend the capital in Italy, and at length the great structure of the Roman empire – its peace and its justice – began to cave in and dissolved through sheer lack of a vital faith to live by, a faith which could support the tradition of classical humanism. You cannot continue for long to believe in man if you cannot believe in something more than man. Belief in a transcendent God is the precondition of any viable humanism. Nor can any society long believe in itself if it has nothing beyond itself to believe in.

It could have been said, no doubt, from a different stand-point, that the Christian faith itself had a share in de-divi-nizing this terrestrial world. It drove out the deities of nature. It dethroned the host of intermediaries – angels and prin-cipalities and powers – that were thought to bridge the gulf between God and man. It declared that the heavenly bodies are not divine beings, that they do not and cannot determine human destinies. Thereby it rid mankind of a terrible burden of fear and dark, irrational superstitions. For though there may be

3

gods many and lords many – even St Paul never quite made up his mind whether there might not be something in them – yet for us there is only one Lord, one Mediator, who gives us direct access to the Father. Yet as Christianity so to speak sprayed antiseptic into that unwholesome, demon-haunted world, many people – like the Mediterranean peasant today – must have felt that they were being left with a rather bleak, depopulated universe, and they wanted still to retain some intermediaries: angels and saints and the prayers of the Mother of God. The old gods did not die; they went underground; many of them still perhaps survive in religious folklore as local saints.

This, however, was popular failure to appreciate the sweep and range of the Christian revolution. For in fact it filled the world with the presence of God. By its faith in Christ as the incarnate Logos, it opened up a sacramental universe in which matter may be the vehicle of God's purpose. (For if Jesus is truly a human being, he was made of the same stuff as the rest of the world, and therefore the whole material order is destined to share in the divine redemption, see Rom. 8.19–23.) In this way science was validated as an element in the life of the Christian church. Far from being devalued, the life of man was restored to its true significance and value in the context of faith in God and eternal life. The world was made a home for the sons of God. Under the tutelage of Christianity England has lived in that faith for a thousand years and accumulated the treasures of Christian humanism.

But humanism today means secular humanism – the claim to believe in man in his own right as a moral and spiritual personality without reference to or belief in God. It sustains many noble and admirable lives and inspires devoted and fruitful social service. It acknowledges ethical values and obligations which Christians and humanists can share together. Christians ought to approach it with a sincere respect. Nevertheless, there is, as we shall see later, a radical self-contradiction at the heart of it. Yet it is this which, for all practical purposes, is now the alternative to the Christian faith. It is widely assumed that man 'come of age' has outgrown and must learn to live without a Christian faith which is no longer credible. 'Christianity could meet our need if it were not, unfortunately, false.' But here we encounter a very surprising paradox. Modern men think of the physical world in a way almost diametrically opposite to that of the Graeco-oriental culture which was the background to early Christianity. Yet starting out from the opposite direction and working by totally different thought-processes, they arrive at the same conclusions as the ancients. Both assume the absence of God from the world. Both conclude that human life is 'absurd'. All the pressures of twentieth-century thought and life tend to exclude belief in the supernatural or in the reality of God.

What has caused the 'progressive withdrawal of divinity' from the twentieth-century world-view is what we now call secularization. A great deal has been written on this subject and we need not discuss it at any length here. A good short definition is the following: secularization is 'the process whereby religious thinking, practice and institutions lose social significance'[3] to become the private affairs of minority groups.

It is popularly assumed that the growth of science is the primary cause of secularization, as it makes religious beliefs no longer credible. But this is a too simplistic explanation. For oddly enough the scientific world-view, which is part of the furniture of the modern mind, coexists quite happily today with all kinds of gross superstition. It has certainly not destroyed credulity. People who shout down the resurrection as something that could not have possibly happened because it 'violates the laws of nature' are prepared to bathe in astrology or spiritism. The causes of scepticism about religion, at least in its traditional Christian form, are complex. But the root cause is probably sociological. It is just that there are so many more people about.

One of the social functions of religion is to supply a framework of meaning for the life of a society as a whole. When a faith is that of an entire community, then religion obviously draws support – though it is not itself derived – from the fact that it is shared and believed by the great majority. (Conversely, non-conformity or 'atheism' is regarded as disruptive

5

and anti-social. Heresy is politically dangerous.) This supplies a 'structure of credibility'. This was possible in the ancient city-states or in the little mediaeval towns, with their small, homogeneous population and the parish church at the centre of the lay-out. But it is not possible in megalopolis. With the enormous increase in population and the consequent break-up of the older communities (due to the mobility of labour) which resulted from the industrial revolution, society has become pluralist and fragmented. There is no longer a uniform community, but a complex of classes and social infra-structures, each with their own sub-cultures and value-systems and, it may be, their own minority beliefs. There is no one faith that sustains the common life. Thus religious thought, practice and institutions, begin to lose their social significance. And this weakens the structure of Christian credibility. As Peter Berger writes, 'This simple sociological fact, and not some magical inexorability of a "scientific" world outlook, is at the basis of the religious plausibility crisis.'[4] Religion has not been 'disproved' by the sciences.

At the same time, it has to be recognized that the movements of thought and life in our own time have tended towards the weakening of belief. For the last half-century, and indeed for that matter ever since the Enlightenment, Western thought has been standing the older philosophies on their heads. Twentieth-century secular man believes – in startling contrast to the ancient thinkers – that the physical universe alone is real and alone the object of real, tested knowledge. He does not believe that there is 'another' world of 'essences' or things-in-themselves underlying the changing phenomena of this world. Scientific knowledge, he thinks, is the only knowledge.

Moreover, the sciences – or so it seems – can give a satisfying account of the world and how it came to be what it is, in their own terms of physical causation, without any recourse to supernatural agency or divine intervention from without. The universe, they assume, runs itself and can be explained from within itself. Thus the God-hypothesis is no longer needed. There is no room left for God in the gaps. Christianity, I should want to say, must agree with that. Science is not concerned with final causes. The questions it asks are how-questions, not why-questions. It cannot and ought not to try to find God in that nexus of secondary causation from which, *ex hypothesi*, he has been excluded; and the scientist would betray his vocation if he cooked his results to make them seem more edifying. *Qua* scientist, he must leave God out. He may, of course, be a profoundly religious man, and his total philosophy is another matter. But for strictly scientific purposes he must work by strictly scientific methods, preserving a rigorous mental objectivity.

For the Christian, all knowledge is the gift of God, through whatever channel it may be communicated. And, as von Hügel taught our generation, religion may sink into superstition if it is not constantly purged by the sciences and the mental discipline which they necessitate. But to accept scientific findings as truth from God within their own limited field is not at all the same thing as to maintain that they tell us the whole truth about the world or that there is no other truth to be known. The sciences can supply only one element in our total understanding of life, though it is an entirely indispensable element in any eventual Christian theology. But their impact on the popular mind has been the conviction that, with all their prestige, they point to a universe from which God is absent.

Meanwhile, the spectacular triumphs of applied science and the technical industrial revolution going forward at ever-accelerating pace are putting control of the world into human hands and eliminating our sense of dependence on supernatural powers not our own. Man, it seems, can now manage the world for himself and, with the knowledge and skill that have now been given to him, mould nature to his own will. Therefore he seems to need God no longer.

In itself, there is nothing un-Christian in the notion that man, now adult and 'come of age', should stand upright on his own feet. Christians believe that it is the will of God to create free spiritual beings capable of freely responding to him. There has therefore been entrusted to men a real, if relative, measure of independence. If there is to be room for men to be men, God must not be (so to speak) too much on top of them. God will not be constantly intervening, telling them hour by hour what to do. Men, endowed with freedom as moral agents, must make their own responsible decisions in God's sight, even if God appears to be absent.

The majority of twentieth-century men interpret this situation as meaning that man now come of age, with his new-won mastery, can get on perfectly well without God. It could almost be said that the twentieth-century axiom is the absence of God from the world of human affairs. Even for many religiously-minded people, God has ceased to be a substantive noun denoting a real, existent personal being, and has become an adjective, a verbal symbol of a religious attitude to life.

But once belief in God has been abandoned, there is nothing left to sustain human values, which can be no more than projections into the void. Stripping to nudity has become a fashion, not only on the stage and the screen, but a mental fashion, a 'modern' way of looking at things. Man is stripped, not least, of his human dignity. Attempting to affirm our humanity by denying anything greater than ourselves, we soon find ourselves trying to discover reality, what we really are, what life is all about, by reducing everything to its lowest terms, taking off its clothes and exhibiting it naked. 'A primrose by the river's brim, a yellow primrose was to him, and it was nothing more.' Nothing more. Nothing but. That is what is the trouble with the modern mind, or the mind that likes to regard itself as modern; its whole trend is incorrigibly reductionist.

Any sentence containing 'nothing but' almost certainly contains a fallacy, if not a cheat, and no educated man ought to allow such a sentence to get past him. For, as a scientist has lately argued, we are beginning to see how 'nothing but' is, if anything, a sign of bankruptcy.

Chemistry is not 'nothing-but' physics, especially the physics of the nucleus; nor is biology 'nothing-but' physics and chemistry; nor is human psychology and sociology 'nothing-but' biology. All these ascriptions, which aspire to subsume the more developed form in terms of the intellectual concepts and experimental approaches which have succeeded at the lower and especially the immediately preceding levels, constitute a mistaken analysis of the modes of investigation which each level of organization of matter renders necessary for its understanding.[5]

It seems probable that the disillusioned cynicism in which so many of our contemporaries appear to find sado-masochistic pleasure, is the fruit of the loss of an ultimate faith in life, and weariness of the burden of being human. 'Things fall apart, the centre cannot hold.' Where there is no ultimate conviction, secular life itself is drained of meaning. 'The trouble is,' said Lord Clark, 'that there is still no centre. The moral and intellectual failure of Marxism has left us with no alternative to heroic materialism, and that isn't enough.'[6] We are left in a moral and spiritual vacuum. 'No centre'; our fathers believed that the world we live in is centred in God, ordered and ruled by God, a world that made sense and in which man's life made sense. The modern secular world is man-centred – and is therefore becoming increasingly thing-centred – and seems to have less and less room for men as what, in their depths, they know themselves to be, that is, personal subjects, or selves. For human life is not self-explanatory. It is always reaching out beyond itself to values and ends which are never fully realized – that is, towards something which transcends man in his total or ultimate environment, in which his selfhood will be fulfilled. If the heavens are empty, if there is nothing there to meet the claim which the self makes on life, then he is condemned to frustration and futility. Human life is 'absurd'; it makes no sense. As David Jenkins shows in his Bampton lectures, without God, man and his world fall apart.[7] Men become alienated from their world, from the social order and from themselves. They distrust life because they distrust the universe which appears to negate what they know they are, and in which there is nothing and nobody that cares. Persons seem to be merely chance by-products of a meaningless and impersonal cosmic process by which, in the end, we are all being eaten up, just as Zeus, in the Greek myth, devoured his offspring. So life seems to be no more than a rat race.

The loss of confidence in the West today is due to this spiritual insecurity. Here is the malaise of our society, the apathy and the lack of directive purpose which threatened to paralyse and devitalize it. There is no fundamental conviction at the heart of it, and there are no commanding non-material values. Heroic materialism is not enough. Moreover, as we were warned long ago, when the house of man's soul is left empty, demonic forces may enter and take possession. It is being proved true in contemporary experience. If suicide is the index of despair, violence may be (as we now know) a symptom of deprivation, that is, of insecurity. It is also a symptom of that flight from reason, with its end-term in social and moral anarchy, which is so alarming a trend in the present world.

What is to fill the spiritual vacuum? It must be remembered that, on the whole, the men and women whose views we hear and quote are the more sophisticated and articulate. But behind the façade of conventional non-belief there are multitudes of men and women who do inarticulately believe in God, or are longing to be able to believe in God and in some absolute moral standard, waiting to be convinced and led. Who or what can rally these silent millions? Surely that is the business of the church? But the church itself shows signs of a loss of nerve, unsure of its mission, uncertain of its own faith, and the great notes of conviction are seldom heard. The church today seems to be introverted, rather than outward looking upon the world, preoccupied with its own internal politics, for ever talking about its public image – which is one of the well-known signs of neurosis – and nervously bent on change for the sake of change. As we know from the study of our own acquaintances, a man who never stops talking about himself, endlessly discussing his symptoms and discontents, and how other people fail to understand him, is almost certainly in for a nervous breakdown. How can the churches themselves recover confidence?

'What the world requires of the Christians,' wrote Camus,' is that they should continue to be Christians.'

I have lived to see nearly everything I care for, and have spent my life trying to serve and set forward, suspect, derided and threatened with destruction. I do not pretend to understand what is happening and I cannot make any attempt to set before you a prediction of the shape of things to come, either in the church or in the world. Sometimes I feel 'a stranger and afraid, in a world I never made'. I am no less perplexed than anyone else. Yet I can still, by the grace of God, believe in the truth of that faith by which I have tried to live. A New Testament writer wrote to some hard-pressed converts about the shaking of all the things that can be shaken, that the things which cannot be shaken may remain. Jesus himself spoke about a house against which the floods descended and the storms blew, but which stood, because it was built on rock.

'Other foundation can no man lay but that which is laid, even Jesus Christ. Let every man take heed what he builds thereon.' I have had to learn, from my reading and in experience, that some of the structures which have been built upon it are 'period' and may not be permanent, and that some of the fabric shows signs of weathering as the acids of modernity bite into it. Our successors may have to reconstruct them with different tools and different materials – which is only to say that the church lives in history. But I have no doubt that the foundation stands.

NOTES

1. Kenneth Clark, *Civilisation*, BBC and John Murray, 1969, p. 347.

2. E. R. Dodds, *Pagan and Christian in an Age of Anxiety*, Cambridge University Press, 1968, who tells us that the phrase was invented by W. H. Auden.

3. Bryan Wilson, *Religion in Secular Society*, Watts, 1966, p. xiv. For more on secularization see my *Secular and Supernatural*, SCM Press, 1969.

4. Peter Berger, *A Rumour of Angels*, Allen Lane: The Penguin Press, 1970, p. 62.

5. A. R. Peacocke, 'Matter in the Theological and Scientific Perspectives', *Thinking about the Eucharist*, SCM Press, 1972, p. 26.

6. Kenneth Clark, op. cit., p. 347.

7. See David E. Jenkins, *The Glory of Man*, SCM Press, 1967, ch. 6.

2 | Who is God and who is man?

What does it mean to be a believing Christian? Clearly not to believe anything and everything that any Christian at any time has believed. Some Christians may have believed all sorts of things which were false or silly or even non-Christian; these, however, were not 'Christian' beliefs in the sense of being constitutive of Christianity, but beliefs held by some Christians on other grounds. What do Christians believe because they are Christians? Out of the whole traditional body of doctrine, some parts of which could perhaps be expendable, what are the fundamental beliefs without which there could be no Christianity? Different readers may give different answers; but I think we should all be agreed in saying that the heart of the Christian faith is the Incarnation.

On Christmas Day God became man – so we read on the posters outside the churches. On the face of it such a statement is so improbable, if indeed not so obviously ridiculous, that the passer-by takes hardly any notice, or just writes it off as the title of a fairy story. It is no doubt a very crude way of putting what is really meant by the Incarnation. But the creed says the same thing in different words. He 'came down from heaven and was made man'. As a symbol of faith I can happily repeat that. It comes out of the heart of Christian experience and affirms that in Jesus we are brought into living relationship with the living God. But in its attempt to spell out the symbol, orthodox, mainstream Christian theology has become involved in statements about the God-Man – statements about the union of two natures, a divine nature and a human nature – which many Christians today find hard to follow and which seem to take Jesus out of history to a world of remote, metaphysical speculation.[1] Perhaps we must start further back than this. What is man's relationship to God? That is the central question of our existence. The Christian claim is that the man Jesus uniquely exhibits that relationship: God's meaning for man and man's meaning for God. Perhaps we may say that essentially Christianity is belief in God and in man through Jesus Christ.

For many reasons, on which I have touched already, God seems to be absent from the world today, and many (including some Christians) find it hard, if not indeed impossible, to believe in God as a real personal being, up there. 'After all, Bishop,' remarked an excellent churchgoer, 'I hope we all believe in a sort of a something.' I hope so, too. But it is rather vague as a faith for a man to live by and die by. Nobody who has been badly hurt, as so many men and women today have been, will be content with such pietistic slush. Desperately they need something to hold on to, someone to trust, in their lostness and despair. It is Job's cry: 'Oh, that I knew where I might find him, that I might know where he dwelt.' Who is God and how can we know him? Is not this what Christianity is about.

In liturgical usage all spoken prayers end with the phrase 'through Jesus Christ our Lord'. It may be a stock conventional formula which serves to round off the rhythm of the sentences. But it is our life, our hope and our salvation. Christians do not, or they should not, doubt that to other peoples and through other faiths some true knowledge of God has been vouchsafed. But for us, in a country which has once been Christianized, there is no going back to other approaches now. This is the point where the frontier is open, the one corridor with light at the end of it.

No man has seen God at any time. He is not part of the world, he is outside the world – we cannot escape from that spatial metaphor – and other than everything that is. Apart from God, nothing could exist, but the world might perish and he would still be God in the mystery of his eternal being, 'dwelling in unapproachable light'. If he is – as to be God he

13

must be – beyond the reach of man's finite mind, we can know only what he wills to disclose to us, communicating himself to the minds of men. We can know him only through his self-revelation. That is what we find in the Bible, and nowhere else. The God of the Bible is a hidden God, not part of the world like the nature-deities, not a tribal god but the Lord of all mankind, to whom the nations are as drops in a bucket; higher than the earth, higher than the heavens, whose ways are not as our ways nor his thoughts as our thoughts. 'To whom will ye liken me?' says the Lord. He is not an object of knowledge among other objects. God *is*, the eternal, initiating Subject. Yet this God, so infinitely far from us, is yet intimately present to us, disclosing himself through his acts in history (as we men show what we are by what we do) and addressing man by his word – that voice that echoes throughout the whole Bible. He spoke to Moses – one of the writers said – 'face to face, as a man speaks to his friend'. This is the God who 'spoke by the prophets', who has 'spoken to us in his Son'.

Revelation is fundamental to Christianity – not the word itself but what it stands for. (Religious words are not sacred cows, and the meaning of words changes with changing times. But as they provide a convenient Christian shorthand, it is well, so far as possible, to retain them.) Christianity starts from God, not from man, and our faith is wholly dependent on what is *given*. But a revelation has to be recognized by the human mind, or nothing has been revealed. If religion is anything but the illusion which Freud – who started by hating God – thought it is, there must be some correspondence, some reciprocity, between God and man. God is the one who communicates with man and man is capable of response to God. That is surely implicit in the biblical statement that God created man in his own image. The climax of this is the life of Jesus, the paradigm of the God and man relationship: on God's side, fullness of self-communication met, on man's side, by entirety of response, in a life of total faith and obedience.

Gethsemane shows the cost of that obedience. He was no automatic Saviour and Revealer. He was not, as it were, simply speaking his lines or effortlessly playing out a role. The ministry opens with the temptation story – temptation (may it have been?) to disobey what Jesus believed to be the Father's will for him, to be ministered to rather than to minister, to impose his own will on the situation; and it cannot have been an isolated incident. ('The devil departed from him for a season', or, as C. H. Dodd translates, 'biding his time'.) He had to fight his way like the rest of us, tempted in all things like as we are – as Hebrews puts it – save without sin. But the 'sinlessness' of Jesus does not mean that he was miraculously immunized from the temptations by which we are assailed, not that he was unable to sin (*non posse peccare*), but that by God's grace he was able not to sin (*posse non peccare*). It was both moral achievement and God's work in him.

Jesus 'grew in wisdom and stature'. In other words, he developed in thought and will – and therefore, presumably, in his appraisals of what was required by changing situations (from the Galilean ministry to the Cross). The incarnation was surely a process, not simply something that occurred when Mary's child was laid in the manger. He was born a baby, not a mature man. But in filial communion with the Father, God was so far the centre of his consciousness – which yet remained genuinely human, limited in knowledge, historically conditioned – that his thought was God's thought and his will the Father's will. He lived God, as Austin Farrer phrased it, or, still better put, God lived him. 'No one knows the Son but the Father, and no one knows the Father but the Son.' He and the Father, he could say, 'are one'. In that climactic reciprocal relation, God and man are brought into real union. But we are not saying that man is 'really' divine or that God 'really' means human goodness. God is God and man is man.

What kind of reality does faith believe in, when it believes in the revelation of God in Jesus Christ? The divine and the human are intimately linked in it. Christian faith believes *at the same time* in a specific event in history and an act of God. Jesus Christ, as the heavenly Lord whom we worship, is *at the same time* an earthly human person . . . What do we mean here by 'at the same time?' How can we conceive of the unity which prevails here between a divine and a human reality? ... Whether or not Christian revelation will be understood and brought to realization in our time depends upon the right or wrong answer to this question.[2]

We must make some attempt towards getting nearer to it.

When Jesus asked the Twelve, 'Will you also go away?', Peter, according to the Fourth Gospel, replied, 'Lord, to whom shall we go?' The West may be drifting away from the Christian faith, but it cannot escape from the spell of its originator. He haunts men still, and they cannot get away from him. Some worship him, while others hate him and are hell-bent to eliminate his influence by pulling down Christian faith and morals. Some are trying to cheapen and sensationalize him or commercialize him into a superstar. He is news. But is the pop Jesus the Christ? There are thousands, of course, including secular humanists, who told him in deep respect and even reverence, with profound admiration for his moral teaching, but stop short of the Christian affirmations. These, they think, are the error that has turned a great teacher and example into a theological conundrum. Christians alone call Jesus Lord and Christ, the Son of God and the Saviour of the world.

Yet how lamentably they have failed to present a compelling Christ to the world – one who, as it has been said, 'subjugates us with the maximum of violence and gentleness'. We have made him a theological lay figure, concealed behind clouds of unreality, not really a human being at all. By reaction, we have tried to eliminate all the mysterious elements in the portrait, reducing him to the measure of our own minds. We have tried to fit him into our preconceptions of what a divine redeemer would be like, instead of submitting ourselves to the evidence. We have made him sickly, mawkish and effeminate; the Old Masters, as someone has remarked, seem to have used a woman as their model – to say nothing about Victorian church windows. But the saccharine Christ of sentimental piety can have nothing to say to a world so hard pressed as ours. Nor can any humanistic presentation account for the sheer fact of Christianity – the faith and commitment of the first believers, the lives of the saints or the deaths of the martyrs. *Why* do

16

Christians believe what they do about him? The answer to that can only be in himself, the man he was and the impact he made. But how far is it possible to recapture that?

It is now merely a truism to say that no one can ever write a 'life' of Jesus. We simply do not have the materials. We know very well that the gospels are not biographies, but rather appeals to faith in the form of a story – and that such books ever came to be produced tells us a great deal about Christianity. They themselves make clear that it is a story about one whose majesty and transcendence far outrange any straight biographical writing. We all know that the gospels are products of the primitive churches, communities of believers, that they are presenting the Christ of faith in their narratives of the life of Jesus, and that there is no going back to recover a Jesus behind the gospels. But what manner of man can he have been to elicit that faith and make that story immortal? This is the 'new quest for the historical Jesus'. And when all the critical work has been assimilated, the gospels do tell us much more about him than all current New Testament scholarship likes to admit. (I can never understand the assumption that the earliest Christians had no interest in the facts about his earthly life. Surely they would have been always eagerly asking for them?) And even if the gospels had not been written, we should still find memories of Jesus in his intrinsic ethos and character, as well as echoes of his actual teaching, in New Testament books earlier than they are. Preserved in the church's corporate tradition, those original memories have never perished. The Lord of the church is the remembered Jesus.

Of course we cannot expect to 'understand' him – the 'most mysterious person that ever was born'. He cannot be fitted into a tidy formula. Others abide our question: he questions us. Nobody could have invented the gospel portrait. He who rejected Napoleonic dreams of the kingdoms of the world and their glory, yet washed the feet of his disciples; so humble he was, yet so imperious; so authoritative, yet so gentle; scorching in holiness, yet the friend of sinners; terrifying in wrath, inexhaustible in compassion; standing over against us as the man from God but identified with us as the man for others; so original, so vital and full of joy, taking upon himself to the uttermost our sins and sorrows, our pains and our despairs. This much at least we know, but who is this?

In a work of highly imaginative fiction, which some Christians may find shocking and even blasphemous, a recent Italian novel (by a believer) has made one more attempt to penetrate the paradox and the mystery of the Christ through the intimations of a poetic vision.[3] Like Blake, the author shatters all the conventional portraits. He has brought to this task the insights of a novelist exploring human situations in depth, his own storm-tossed spiritual odyssey and a vivid awareness of the predicament – the rebellions and despair – of 'modern man'. This life, he says, 'stands above hagiography and the narration of facts, it tends to become a *summa* of human arguments and passions'. He breaks away from the too narrow moralism and too restrictedly 'religious' content to which too much preaching and teaching has been limited, to show us all human experience mirrored there. 'He died to make us good' – but is that all? He did not reveal religion, he revealed God.

We cannot read off a loving God from the world. That faith can no longer be taken for granted. It was 'killed in action' on the Somme and cremated at Auschwitz and Hiroshima. Only this strange man with the cross can give it to us, in his life and death and resurrection. All our obstinate questionings meet in him. In a sterner sense than the Christmas hymn knew, 'the hopes and fears of all the years are met' in this challenging, suffering, loving man, and the pains and bewilderments of our tragic world are seen to be reconciled with an ultimate meaning. Through him we are given a presence in our lostness, hope in the abyss of our despair, victory won out of failure and defeat, release from the solitary self-confinement which in religious language is called sin, courage to be ourselves and a trust strong enough to overcome the fear of dying. If that is not what we mean by faith in God – or at any rate part of what we mean – what is? It is given to us 'through Jesus Christ our Lord'. In him, Santucci concludes, is 'the key to the continuation or evaporation of faith on the earth'.

This does not rest on a theory but on a life, lived in an

actual, concrete situation, a life many-faceted in its expressions and reactions to manifold experience, yet integrated into one perfect whole of creative goodness and healing love. This is something absolute and final – the divine life, exhibited not in word only but in deed and in truth, in this one man. This is what makes it possible to believe in the divine compassion at the heart of things, and a God to whom persons are dear.

It was not, of course, till after the resurrection that the 'Christian' interpretation of Jesus was born in the minds of the disciples. The resurrection created the community which at once began to proclaim the gospel – at first, it seems, in a most rudimentary form.[4] Indeed we may say that the church and the preaching – the *koinōnia* and the *kerygma* – are in effect two aspects of the same thing. But the point of the resurrection appearances is that the risen Lord who appeared to his followers *was* the Jesus whom they had known in Galilee. What was given to them was a new understanding of what they had found in him during his earthly ministry; and the gospels were written, as C. F. D. Moule remarks, 'to show how the pre-resurrection situation gave rise to the post-resurrection situation'.[5] They would not have worshipped the risen Christ as Lord had they not found something in Jesus of Nazareth which they now came to recognize as the presence of God. With all his evident discontinuity, the risen Christ was continuous with Jesus.

In spite of widespread popular opinion, Jesus did not claim that he was God Almighty. Anyone who did that would be mentally deranged. (There are plenty of people in psychiatric wards who will tell you that they are God, or Jesus Christ; and Nietzsche ended his days in an asylum.) Indeed, he expressly refused any such suggestion: 'Why do you call me good? Only God is good.' There seems to be no doubt that he did claim a unique insight into the mind of God. He claimed a unique standing with the Father and spoke 'with authority' in the name of God. He made a total demand on his followers with no hesitation about his right to make it. He exercised the forgiveness of sins – to the scandal of his Jewish critics. The most theological of the gospels concentrates on the concept of the Son who knows the Father as no one else can know him. But he never said that he *was* the Father. He is recorded as saying, 'My Father is greater than I'. (The cheap slogan 'There is no God but Jesus', based on a flagrant misuse of the saying, 'He who has seen me has seen the Father', trivializes the majesty of God.) The Jesus presented to us in the gospels is not a man disguised as a god (the classical dictionary is stiff with those), nor what the Greeks called a divine man (*theios anēr*), possessed by a spirit of which he was the mouthpiece, but genuinely human, a man 'in the ordinary sense of the word' – though by no means an ordinary man. 'Never man spoke,' they said, 'as this man.' It is clear that he was urgently conscious of being charged by God with a unique mission, But whether he thought of himself as Messiah must now be regarded as at least uncertain; Son of man was his own self-chosen title, though we do not and cannot know just what he meant by that. It is vain for us to attempt to psychologize him or try to penetrate into his inner consciousness. And, in any case,

The Christian faith is not a belief that Jesus entertained certain ideas, which therefore must be true; it is rather the conviction, grounded in the concrete realities of the Church's life (including the memory of Jesus himself), that his career was the central element in a divine and supremely significant event.[6]

It must be obvious that the disciples did not think of their master as God. To them, as Jews, that would have been blasphemy. Again and again they 'got it all wrong' and completely misunderstood what he was teaching them. But they found in him something that passed their understanding, which was (as we say) altogether out of this world, something trans-human and supernatural, some enhanced awareness of divine reality. They trusted him with an implicit trust and obeyed him with an unquestioning obedience. For his sake they abandoned all that men hold dear. To be with him was worth more than all the world to them. To be with Jesus seemed to be very heaven.

All that was shattered by the crucifixion. If the God whom Jesus had taught them to trust had allowed him to be rejected and put to death, it had been a ghastly mistake after all; and we can hardly exaggerate their despair. But when Jesus came to them living and victorious, it was clear that God had accepted and vindicated him, that the living and true God was committed to him, that God, and no less, had been present and at work in him. It was God who had come near to them in Jesus. God had made him both Lord and Christ; and to him they were now impelled to offer worship. But how could the worship of Christ be reconciled with their uncompromising Jewish monotheism? In a new form the question arose, Who is he? How is Jesus the Christ related to God? That was where Christian theology began, and in effect all subsequent Christian 'doctrine' is the ongoing attempt of the church to answer it.

Lord, in Greek (kyrios), can mean anything in a series from a title like 'Sir' to the Lord God Almighty. It is the word used in the Septuagint, the Greek Old Testament, to translate the ineffable name of the Lord Yahweh; and at least some overtones of that meaning must surely have been resonant in their minds. Jesus is the Christ, God's final word in history, and that promised new age has therefore already begun. Jesus is Lord, who both claims our allegiance and brings God into the lives of men. For my own part, I could rest content with that, leaving the fuller interpretation open. Anyone who can say Jesus is Lord, has heard the heartbeats of the Christian faith.

Yet the thought of the church was bound to venture further than that. The New Testament offers a torrent of various phrases – metaphorical and sometimes mythological – in attempts to convey what the Lord Jesus meant to those who were now committed to him by faith. These are foundation documents for the church, for they bring us nearest to first-hand experience and so mediate that faith to us. It does not follow that for all time the church is tied to those particular phrases which are – as we must recognize – conditioned by a particular cultural situation. Jesus is far greater than any words we use about him, and he broke through all those tentative Christologies, which one after another are discarded. The New Testament writers, broadly speaking, are content to describe him in biblical terms of function rather than in terms

21

of his essential being, to ask, What has he done for us? rather than, Who is he? But the latter had to be thought out philosophically; and that was the work of the Greek theologians.

The great language about 'coming down from heaven' must, of course, be accepted frankly as symbolic – it would be nonsense as literal description; Jesus did not descend from above the bright blue sky. Some Christians today regard it as too misleading and want to see it rewritten in different words. If better words can be found, let us have them. But the creeds are not meant to be down-to-date theology; they are meant to be statuesque; they are symbols. And I do not think any other words could do nearly so well what these are intended to do. They guard against any facile adoptionism and throw the whole emphasis on the divine initiative. Jesus was not a Man who became a God, who after death became a divine personage and was adopted to be a son of God, like the *divi Caesares* of the Roman empire. What is vital to any Christian interpretation is that this life was willed and 'sent' by God, originating in the divine will. As St John puts it, he 'came forth from God'. If it was an expression of the divine will, then it could be said that it was 'purposed before the foundation of the world', or, as in the prologue of the Fourth Gospel, that 'he was eternally in relation to God'.

For who can bring God into the life of man except God himself? God is not a something that can be conveyed by an appointed messenger, any more than grace is a thing, a substance, that can be laid on through appropriate channels – it is God's free and unmerited self-giving. When we speak of Jesus the Christ as the mediator between God and man, we half-suggest that he was a kind of go-between, not himself personally either, which rules out the essential Christian faith. If the Christ brings God into human life, then he can be no less than the incarnate Logos. He must himself be God, both God and man. There is the central mystery and paradox, echoed at folk-song level in the carols, of which we can offer no 'explanation'.

The classical formulation of Christian thinking, after the long Christological debates, was the *homoousion* of Nicaea.

Jesus is not 'like' God, but identical with God. The God who is immanent in the whole creation is here 'personally' disclosed in act, in the fullest measure in which the being of God can be expressed in terms of human experience. When we affirm the divinity of Christ, what fundamentally we are asserting is that in him we encounter the living God – not the private deity of a Christian cultus, but the one true God, maker of heaven and earth and of all things visible and invisible. In other words, it is really a statement not so much about the nature of Christ as about the mysterious power that runs the universe. We think of him best when we think of Jesus. What we find there is not a vast abstraction but the one whom, because of him, we call Love and Father. The light of the knowledge of the glory of God is given to us in the face of Jesus Christ.

I do not suggest that the seeker must accept the full 'ortho-dox' doctrinal interpretation before he can venture to call himself a disciple. 'We do not know where you are going,' said sceptical Thomas, 'and how can we know the way?' The answer was, 'I am the way.' Take my hand and come with me. You will find out the answer as we go along. Many a man who does not believe in God and protests that he does not and cannot believe, has trusted Jesus enough to go with him, following through the darkness of doubt, and has found in that following the light of God.

The Nicene Creed can never be expendable. It stands as the magnificent affirmation of what is implied in Christian faith and experience. Yet is is stated in terms of a philosophy which changed cultural forms have now made obsolete. We cannot today think in terms of 'substance'. We may have to find other words and other categories – less abstract, more personal and dynamic – in which to communicate it to our own world.[7]

The trend of western society as we know it is towards the subordination of personal values to technical and economic processes. Man, who is able now to control nature and estab-lish his rightful dominion over it, is in real danger of being himself de-humanized. Christians and humanists are alike con-cerned to re-establish man in his humanness. At a time when all human values are at risk they ought to be working together as partners, not regarding one another as rivals and attacking one another's positions. The church is in the world to save the world, not merely to score points for its own beliefs. Yet it can make no effective contribution if it starts by accepting the humanist assumptions, or enter on any humanist-Christian dialogue by abandoning the Christian position and saying, 'We can talk about God another time.' For if so, it will not be a dialogue at all. Christians and humanists both believe in man, but they believe for very different reasons and understand him in very different ways. (So Christians and humanists both believe in freedom, yet they do not really agree about what it is.) The Christian believes in man as a child of God, and his understanding of man is therefore God-centred. God is the *prius* of Christian anthropology. However much they may learn from the natural sciences and however much 'secular' information they may (rightly) bring to bear on the human problem, Christians must be thinking as Christians, that is, from a Christocentric point of view. When they speak of man, they mean man as revealed in Christ, in his true relationship to God, and therefore to his world and his fellow-men. It is futile to go on saying that 'deep down' Christians and humanists really mean the same thing. The suggestion is both wounding and untrue.

The humanist and the 'liberal' understanding is confined in a strictly human frame of reference. Man is taken as self-sufficient and self-explanatory, and he is assumed to be naturally perfectible. He fails, if he does, only through adverse circumstances; change them, and man will enter into his glory. And now, at long last, it is in our power to change them. New social techniques are now available, science can now act as fairy godmother. So this creed tends to be strongly optimistic and engenders visions of man-made utopias – more knowledge, more education, more science and yet more technology, fewer restraints and better welfare services, and man will be able to realize his humanness. 'These things shall be: a loftier race/than e'er the world hath known shall rise.' (Time was when we used to sing that in our churches and think we were singing about the kingdom of God!) The climax comes with 'Jerusalem' by massed choirs.

Christians ought never to speak disrespectfully about any programme, from whatever source, that may help to liberate and enrich man's life, simply because it is not of Christian origin. And this is a fine emancipating ideal which has summoned many to dedicated service. But any Christian can see what is the matter with it. As Reinhold Niebuhr taught our generation, it simply leaves out the fact of 'original sin'. And as these utopian expectations fail and the forces against man seem to be gathering strength, some even of the noblest spirits fall down into cynicism and disillusion, if not into total despair and embittered anarchism. The suicidal conclusion is near at hand that the human experiment has somehow failed and the effort is no longer worth keeping up.

But though speeches professing that scientific optimism are still being offered on a hundred platforms, there is already a strongly period ring in them. There are signs of a growing suspicion now that science is not so much the Messiah as the anti-Christ. For is it not science that powers and directs that vast network of interlocking mechanisms by which, in any industrialized society (and that will soon mean every society), persons are being so rapidly depersonalized? Is it not likely that selective breeding, biological engineering and so forth – controlled by pundits who claim omniscience, who *know* what kind of men ought to exist – will effectively rob us of our humanness and turn humanity into an Animal Farm? And is not this a threat even more alarming than that of destroying the race by a nuclear holocaust? It begins to look as though science were something too dangerous to be safely left to scientists. Must it not be brought under human and moral control?

But here we uncover the ground of the misgivings about science as saviour from our predicament. At a time when people are desperately seeking for some meaning, some value, in our existence, science appears to have nothing to contribute. It is not concerned with values and meanings. Indeed, they are excluded from its purview. At best it can only observe man from without; but man knows himself from within. (This is the valid protest of existentialism.) It seems that not all the sciences added together can tell us what it is to be human. So it is now being asked again whether, after all, religious intuitions ought not to be taken more seriously in our efforts to answer the question, What is man?

The discussion about science and value needs treatment at greater length and depth than can possibly be attempted here. I can offer only one or two summary pointers to it. Science as such cannot discover values – which can never be found by methods of induction – any more than it can discover God. Both are excluded from its field of reference. But that does not mean that the scientific world-view must exclude values from the total universe or from its presentation of human life – for man lives by values and meanings, and the most scientific account of anything, as Austin Farrer remarked, is the true account. The world of the sciences is not the whole world; it is a highly sophisticated abstraction from the totality of our environment, which is clearly qualitative as well as quantitative, and includes – to go no further – the scientist, with his loves and hates, his manifold aims and interests. And, as we have noted already, the investigator is himself involved in his investigations, and therefore try as he may to rule out the 'personal factor', inevitably brings to them his own values and presuppositions. It looks as though the philosophy of science were now beginning to enter upon a new phase. The apparently 'inhuman' trend of science is one more illustration of the fact that once belief in God has been abandoned and the centre no longer holds, things fall apart and all our thinking and knowledge becomes fragmentated. One fruitful task of theology today, as is being found in some of the universities, is to mediate between specialized departments and bring 'Arts' and sciences into some kind of wholeness. It is the Christian doctrine of man as at once child of nature and child of God which gives to the sciences their rightful place as a ministry subserving human values in the divinely ordered plan of creation. It is, in the end, only belief in God which validates either our science or our humanness.

But there is, of course, no Christian account of man which is just an alternative to the scientific. However exalted the claims that we make for man, that is the foundation on which we must always build. Man is, no doubt, unique in the whole creation: all his bodily and mental processes are those of man, not of pre-human species. Yet we know that we are the products of evolution, made of the same primal world-stuff as animal, vegetable and mineral.

The level of organization of matter which we call man is thus as much and as little describable in terms of the physics and chemistry of his constituent atoms and molecules as any other organism.[8]

We do not make any account of man more 'Christian' by trying to minimize his materiality. God made man out of dust of the earth. The world is so constituted that in the end persons emerge out of inorganic matter – that is part of the wonder of creation. But what is it that makes human beings human, distinguishing them from their fellow-creatures?

The popular Christian answer to that has been that man has a soul but his cats and dogs have not. Some Christians are afraid that biochemistry, neurophysiology and the rest will end by eliminating the 'soul' and leaving merely a bundle of physical reflexes. But such fears rest in the end on a false antithesis. The idea of a separable soul which, as it were, inhabits a bodily organism and therefore, being naturally immortal (a word seldom found in the New Testament), survives the dissolution of the body, is Greek rather than Christian in origin. It is indeed diametrically opposed to the doctrine of man contained in the Old Testament. The Bible sees man as a psycho-physical unity and works with no dualism of soul and body. (The meaning of 'soul' in the Creation myth is what we should now call a living organism.) When a man dies, therefore, all of him dies.

Beyond the rejection of absolute materialism – that is, the actual identification of mind with discharges in brain cells – Christian thought is probably not committed to any one particular answer to the mystery of the body–mind relationship, and perhaps there is no quite satisfactory answer. (When Professor Ryle coined his famous phrase that there is no ghost in the machine, undergraduates at the time seized upon it as a high-level 'disproof' of Christianity. 'There you are, there aren't any souls; we are merely mechanisms!' Ryle was in fact saying nothing of the kind.) But it would be making a bad mistake, alike in science and in theology, if it tried to maintain that man is pure spirit. If, as seems likely, the scientific account points to complete psycho-somatic unity, that will, as it happens, be more in line with the Bible than the allegedly more enlightened theory derived from Greek and oriental philosophy.

Souls are not something that we have, but what we are or what we are becoming – moral and spiritual personalities. What we mean in saying that man 'has a soul' is that what is distinctively human about us, what makes man man, is his self-transcendence, his outreach towards values, aims and ideals ever beyond him and not themselves the resultants of any physical process – that is, his openness to the supernatural. But we never cease to be biological organisms. We are not physical when we eat our dinner and spiritual when we say our prayers – if that were true, what could we say about the eucharist? – any more than Jesus himself was speaking and acting at one time as man, at another time as God. (I was taught something like that when I was young, but of course it makes nonsense of Christianity.) We are always 'at one and the same time' both at once. We live at the intersecting of two planes, the physical and the metaphysical, the empirical and the supernatural. We can never find self-understanding within the closed frontiers of naturalism.

Christian faith will, of course, want to say more: that we cannot give any true account of man or understand what we really are, if we leave out that relationship with God which is what constitutes our distinctive humanness. In other words, any true anthropology must be worked out in a theological context – the reverse of the programme now being pressed upon us. In Jesus we see that to be fully human is to be rightly related to God, and that is precisely what none of us now are. We are sinners – that is, we are estranged from God – and some are in active rebellion against him – and so from our world, our fellows and ourselves. We are alienated from our environment – and in man's environment man himself is the chief factor – because we are alienated from God. Christianity takes a more tragic view of man than that of twentieth-century progressivism: it does not think he is naturally perfectible. Yet it is infinitely more optimistic. Christians believe that the coming of Jesus Christ has changed the whole human situation by rectifying that false relationship, so that we and our world can be reconciled with God, and by opening possibilities of living hitherto unrealized and unimagined.

NOTES

1. E.g. 'Who, although he be God and man, yet he is not two but one Christ: God of the substance of the Father, begotten before the worlds, and man of the substance of his Mother, born into the world: equal to the Father as touching his Godhead and inferior to the Father as touching his manhood' (Athanasian Creed). This is theologically impeccable, but what are perplexed Christians to make of it today?

2. Heinz Zahrnt, *The Question of God*, Collins, 1969, pp. 205f.

3. Luigi Santucci, *Wrestling with Christ*, Collins, 1972.

4. See the extremely primitive exposition offered in Acts 3. 19.

5. C. F. D. Moule, *The Phenomenon of the New Testament*, SCM Press, 1967, p. 73.

6. John Knox, *The Death of Christ*, Collins, 1959, p. 124.

7. Hugh Montefiore, 'Towards a Christology for Today', in A. R. Vidler (ed.), *Soundings*, Cambridge University Press, 1962; see also John A. T. Robinson, *The Human Face of God*, SCM Press, 1973, an important book published after this chapter was written.

8. A. R. Peacocke, *Science and the Christian Experiment*, Oxford University Press, 1971, p. 141.

3 | The question of truth

Relativity with everything?

'Give me somewhere to stand,' said Archimedes, 'and I will lift the world with my lever.' It was the justifiably proud claim made for a new technical discovery, as it has since been made for many another. A new power had been put into human hands, and there seemed to be no limit to its uses. It might turn the world upside down. Possibly: but where was he to find a stance? In principle it might now be possible to hoist Mount Ossa from its foundations by basing his lever on the top of Pelion. But where could Archimedes find a stance, a fixed point, for lifting the world itself? Only by going outside the world of which both he and his lever were parts. In the world there can be no absolute point of leverage.

Translate that from physical into mental terms, and you are not far from the central question which is now challenging Christian faith and morals. It is, of course, the question of relativism. Many thinkers in all generations have claimed to have discovered the master-key, whether in science or in philosophy, which would unlock the secrets of the universe. But with changing historical conditions they have all been blown by the winds of change, one after another, down the stream of time. Is there any permanent master-key available?

The Greeks thought of the world in terms of being. What were real, for them, were the eternal essences, the ideas or constitutive forms of things – what makes anything the thing it is – lying behind contingency and change. We think of the world as process, as becoming. In a universe that is constantly evolving, of which we ourselves are parts and products, where can we stand to find any explanation? Still more, in an Einsteinian cosmology which has no centre, no 'here' or 'there', in which everything is involved in relativity, where can we hope to insert our mental leverage? Our fathers believed in a static, predictable universe governed by immutable 'laws of nature' and the mathematics of Newtonian physics. They thought that these laws were normative, were *laws*, in the sense that they were imposed on the cosmos and might not be and could not be disobeyed. ('Laws that never can be broken/for their guidance he has made.') How then, they asked, could there be any room for miracles as 'violations of the laws of nature' or indeed for any revealed religion at all, which was held to be bound up with the miraculous? For miracles in that sense 'do not happen' (Matthew Arnold). If the laws are really immutable, they cannot happen. (So Hume, who argued, however, that there are no 'laws'; they are only associations of ideas.) That was the difficulty of the mid-Victorians. It seemed to them, in their agonized debates, that science did indeed provide a key, but that if you used it, religion was locked out.

Our difficulty is almost the opposite. We have learnt that the so-called laws of nature are not laws, determining the course of things, but are in fact scientific hypotheses, and we know that these are constantly in revision. The laws of nature change from month to month and from one generation to another, as new facts are experimentally discovered which will not fit into earlier hypotheses. New 'laws' must therefore be suggested and tested out by mounting new experiments, devising new models, framing new hypotheses, which in due course will again have to be revised. So we find ourselves now in a fluid, open universe, far more alive and with richer potentialities than earlier generations had understood, in a world that is always bringing forth something new. But at this point we run into another question. Can there, then, be any finality to our knowledge, any fixed point from which we can account for or interpret the ever-flowing stream of energy? Scientists themselves are the last people to claim or expect to have any final answers. They *want* their hypotheses to be overthrown, so that they can be led or driven to try others. It is of the very nature of science that it

31

cannot stop still, cannot rest content in any position which it has so far occupied. It is an endless quest, not an answer. Is there still, then, no stance for Archimedes? Is all knowledge tentative and provisional? Must we have relativity with everything?

For thousands of years it has been religion which has claimed to be in possession of the key and to offer a stance 'outside' the world, in the sense that it rests, or is believed to rest, on realities which are not empirical, not immersed in the flux of space-time. All the higher religions make that claim, and among them particularly Christianity, which claims to offer a 'final' revelation, and is indeed irrevocably committed to it by its faith in Christ as the incarnate Logos.

The New Testament, in various figures of speech, attributes to him a cosmic significance (to those with a Jewish background, the very title Christ implies that). St John opens his gospel by saying that the story which he is going to tell reveals to us how the world is made. In him, says St Paul, all things consist. Revelation 5 puts it in pictorial form in the scene of the adoration of the Lamb, who alone has prevailed to break the seals and open the book of the secrets of the universe. Here we have knowledge given by God himself, derived from the one whom 'the world does not contain'. Here – Christians have maintained – is the truth. Here is something final and authoritative, given to us by a divine revelation not exposed to the changing fashions of thought – and to this, our grandparents would have added, set forth to us in infallible propositions dictated by God himself, in the Bible. Here we have the permanent and reliable stance for which purely secular knowledge seeks in vain. Round that centre, or on that projection, we can plot what William Temple called, in his younger days, a Christian map and construct a Christian world-view.

But today that stance, too, has become precarious. Not only does the prevailing philosophy discount the idea of a metaphysical world-view, but the claim to any divine revelation is now exposed to damaging attack by a relativistic attitude to all knowledge. Religion itself has now been hit by relativism.

The dangerous challenge to Christian belief comes now not so much from the physical as from the behavioural and human sciences, and especially from sociology, which is thought to supply new weapons for scepticism.

As a human and social phenomenon, religion is clearly related to social structures. The correlation between religion and class first came to light in the census of 1851, and a great deal of work has been done on the subject since then. It can be shown how the various infra-structures of which any society is composed throw up or 'project' religious beliefs and attitudes (some of which may of course be anti-religious) which reflect their own emotional needs and their own relative structural situations. They are all, it seems, sociologically conditioned, and no absolute claims can be made for any of them. Sociology, says Peter Berger,' raises the vertigo of relativity to its most furious pitch'.[1] When it is the religion of a whole society, religion provides the mystique for that society. 'It is always at least an expression of a society's moral unity, and it lends to that unity a cosmic and universal significance and justification.'[2] In a uniform and closely compact society, all alike share the same religious beliefs and acknowledge the same standards of behaviour. That was so in the tribe and the ancient village and perhaps in the mediaeval small town, which was the background of St Thomas Aquinas. But in the fragmented, pluralist society which emerged from the industrial revolution, different groups live in different worlds, whose beliefs and ways of living are conditioned by their varying structures and affiliations. 'We are no longer a single culture which can be instructed by sermons. We are not bound by commandments but by loyalties.'[3]

Religion thus becomes one among many other forms of men's response to their environment. The 'world' of the believer and theologian becomes just one 'world' among many others. What he believes seems therefore to be relative and conditioned throughout by social pressures. 'We' believe one thing and 'they' believe another. Is the one belief valid for them and the other for us? How can we test the validity of either? For anyone who proposes to adjudicate will himself be conditioned no less than they are.

We seem to be sinking into a frightful nightmare of inconsequence and irrationality. 'Vortex is king.' Relativity takes all. We are in a world of paralysing scepticism, where all statements are equally true and all, therefore, equally false, in which indeed there is neither truth nor falsity, no absolute values, no mental stance. All truth, we are frequently told, is relative. Philosophy students in their first year tend to get drunk on this witches' brew: I did myself; and at this stage it seems to them a mark of sophistication and maturity. But their education will have been sadly shallow, if before they go down they have not seen through it.

For just at this point relativity oversteps itself. If anyone tells me that all that is relative, he is tacitly making one exception, namely the statement that all truth is relative; for this, he defiantly maintains, is true, is the absolute and final truth; anybody who does not agree with that is either dishonest or mentally sub-normal, blinded by outworn dogmas, and the like. But on what possible grounds can he base that claim? How can he demand that this statement should be exempted? For he, too, has been socially conditioned. His dislike for his father, who was a convinced believer; his devotion to a 'rationalist' uncle who introduced him to free-thinking circles; some prejudice which a tutor handed on to him; his failure to get his degree in philosophy – any such factors may lie behind his assertion. But he simply cannot have it both ways.

If we take relativity to its furthest limits, we reach solid ground behind the frontier.

When everything has been subsumed under the relativizing categories in question . . ., the question of truth reasserts itself in almost pristine simplicity. Once we know that all human affirmations are subject to scientifically graspable socio-historical processes, *which affirmations are true and which are false?* (italics original). . . . What follows is *not*, as some of the early sociologists of knowledge feared, a total paralysis of thought. Rather, it is a new freedom and flexibility in asking questions of truth.[4]

Radical theologians, for example, observe that New Testament thought and language reflects a social and cultural situation which is not that of the twentieth-century world and that therefore the 'modern mind' cannot take them. Before we can swallow them, they must be demythologized. But the modern mind is no less conditioned by its own social and cultural situation. By what right do we claim its pontifications as ultimate? 'Sociology frees us from the tyranny of the present.' Sociologists can provide the evidence that certain forms of belief or disbelief are characteristic of twentieth-century Englishmen or of certain sub-groups in contemporary society. But the question has still to be asked. Do we agree with them? Do we think that these opinons are true? That cannot be answered by sample opinion polls – any more than the presentation by the media of prevalent kinds of human behaviour will answer the question how people ought to behave. Neither truth nor good can be synthesized. Both are ultimate, irreducible. The concept of truth is the *prius* of any thinking. We cannot think about anything at all if we do not accept the law of contradiction: a thing cannot be both A and not-A. All-out relativism is self-defeating.

In the end, therefore, to quote Beyer again, 'relativizing analysis, in being pushed to its final conclusion, bends back upon itself. The relativizers are relativized, the debunkers are debunked.' So we come back again to the question of truth, and the rational supports for the Christian faith.

Faith and reason

The fundamental question before the churches is not that about their institutional structures, with which they are so unhealthily preoccupied. It is whether Christianity is true. But what can that mean and how could it be substantiated? Any attempt to answer that question is bound to take us into deep waters and involve some philosophical discussion. For it is widely held now that philosophy rules out the truth of any religious statement. In a book of this kind I can do no more than offer some basic, elementary materials. But it is a question that cannot be evaded by the educated twentieth-century Christian who wants to love God with all his mind.

If we accept the scientific world-view, is there any real place for theology? Is not 'religious knowledge' bogus knowledge, as fifty per cent of the RE class suspect? Undeniably it can give us information about what people believe and the way they worship. But that is descriptive science, not theology. If it asserts that these beliefs are true – that they tell us something about what is real – has it not overstepped the boundaries of knowledge and left rational argument behind? When the first 'new' universities were founded, theology was rigorously excluded as a proper subject of academic discipline. It was then regarded as dealing with questions which were rather matters of private opinion than of considered rational enquiry, and indeed as being in some way irrational and incapable of objective verification. But it is, surely, a most significant fact that today, in almost all the universities, including both the Victorian red-bricks and the numerous post-war foundations, there are vigorous departments of theology, and that the demand for them is growing. The question of God is no longer banned from the field of knowledge or the quest for truth. And of course, Christianity, no less than the sciences, presupposes faith in a rational universe.

What I have to try to do in the next few pages is to show that belief in God is not irrational. There is no antithesis between faith and reason. At the same time, it has to be frankly admitted that reason alone cannot generate faith or establish the reality of God.

But how, then, can theology do its job at all? It can hardly begin if it cannot assume, or demonstrate, that there is a Subject, a reality, to which or to whom its statements refer, so that we can say God is good, all-wise, immortal and so forth – in other words, that God does exist. ('Before you ask me to believe in God you must prove to me that there is a God to believe in.') But that, it seems, is precisely what it cannot do. No man has seen God at any time. What the word God means by definition is infinite self-subsistent Being, beyond the reach of man's finite mind, who is thus for ever in some sense unknown. We can form no concept of what it is to be God. He *is*: 'I am that I am.' The Hebrews would not pronounce the sacred name. We cannot describe God, for description is of objects that can be identified, and God is not an object that can be identified as one among other objects of knowledge. He is the source and ground of all that exists and therefore the presupposition of all knowledge. Our logic and our language are structured so as to deal with finite realities; and God is not a finite reality, in series, as it were, with other realities. Yet we cannot speak about God at all without seeming to make him a finite object. Thus theology seems, from its very nature as God-talk, to be involved in self-contradiction.

If we think of God as one object among others or even as a subject who can be regarded as also one object among others, we are treating him as a finite being – that is, as what he is not. But how are we to avoid doing this if we are to think of him at all?[5]

If God transcends all finite knowledge, then he is, in his being, a 'hidden' God. He cannot be contained in a logical argument; he is, as the creed says, 'incomprehensible' – that is, incapable of definition. There is no human mental apparatus which can prove or demonstrate God's existence – or, by the same token, disprove it either. God, to be God, remains for ever unknown. Clouds and darkness are round about him. He abides, in the mystery of his eternal being. But does that mean that nothing can be known about him? For in that case faith could be merely a leap in the dark, would indeed be no more than anybody's guess. Nor could it have any bearing on real life. If 'transcendence' means that in his very nature God is wholly and totally unknowable, it would seem to make him totally irrelevant; he might just as well, so to speak, not be there. For all practical purposes it could make no difference – and that is what the popular mind suspects in the current revolt against a transcendent God.

But 'the structure of religious experience is such that what is essentially unknown is also actually known'.[6] Religion, and Christianity in particular, rests on the claim that God has made himself known through his self-disclosure to man in revelation, and that is the presupposition of the whole Bible – for, contrary to popular belief, the Bible offers no proof of God's existence – and I need not repeat here what I have said already. But religion itself requires both a God who meets man and makes himself known to man, and also one who is infinitely beyond us – 'a God far off, not a God at hand' – who, though he is known to us, yet remains unknown. Religion has its being in mystery. Christianity lives in a daylight world, not among the dark gods of the underworld. Yet it is a response to the ultimately mysterious, which is what all religion is about. A God about whom we knew all that there is to be known would be part of the world, limited and conditioned by realities other than himself, not the object of religous awe and worship. One whom the finite mind could comprehend would not be the Lord God Almighty in any sense that matters to religion. But if we say that, does it mean that faith and worship can never have any rational justification?

For nearly a thousand years the Christian West, with the thought of Plato and Aristotle behind it, had assumed that reason can know the timeless forms and realities underlying the changing flux of things (indeed that of these alone can there be true knowledge), and could thus discern the structuring of the cosmos. From this knowledge of how the world 'really' is, it could argue to the reality and the nature of the unchanging reality which sustained it. Thus it seemed that by rational enquiry a line of argument lay from the world to God. The Schoolmen[7] even believed that by these methods one could 'prove' the reality of God and of the fundamental Christian beliefs. So there was built up the magnificent intellectual structure which was the mental cathedral of Christendom – the vast, rational system of Christian theism. This was metaphysics or natural theology,[8] which provided the rational support scaffolding for the intuitions of Christian faith. But, as all students of the subject know, that monument of thought was destroyed by the critical revolution in philosophy headed by Hume in Britain and Kant in Germany, which involved the demolition of metaphysics and the old-style natural theology. And of course the famous 'proofs' went down with it.

The proofs are now generally discredited and have little value for Christians today. But they were the work of extremely acute minds, and some understanding of what they were trying to do and of the arguments which they employed can throw a strong light on some of our present problems. Let me therefore briefly suggest why they failed and why any attempted proof of the kind is bound to fail. As John Hick has recently pointed out, there is a 'catch' in them from the start. For they take for granted what they set out to 'prove'. They presuppose the Christian belief in God and can only succeed on the basis of that belief. They were thought up to give Christians confidence, and can never bring conviction to unbelievers.

St Thomas Aquinas lists the traditional proofs in his classical discussion of the Five Ways.[9] He rejects Anselm's 'ontological' proof, which is an attempt to prove by pure thought, without any appeal to factual evidence, the necessity of a necessary being, whose 'essence' necessitates his existence. What it comes to is something like this. You can say 'If angels exist, they are immaterial'. There is no necessity why they must exist; if they do, it is a contingent existence. Thus it is not self-contradictory or illogical to say, 'Angels do not exist'; whether they do or not is a question of fact. But you cannot say 'If a necessary being exists', for if it is possible that he does not exist, then he is not a necessary being. If by God we mean self-subsistent Being, not dependent on anything other than himself, and therefore contingent, then it is not logically possible to think that he might be non-existent.

The others are all, as I have said, attempts to argue to the reality of God from the constitution of the universe – just as the eighteenth-century Age of Reason derived the 'evidences' of Christianity, not from the Bible or any form of theological reasoning, but from nature. (Think of the now notorious 'Paley's *evidences*'.) Science, it was supposed, could prove religion. Now St Thomas concludes the arguments by saying: 'And this is what everybody calls God.' But they don't, unless they believe in God already.

Take, for example, the 'cosmological' proof, which in principle embraces the whole group. The argument runs that a contingent universe in which everything is finite and limited and everything is dependent on something else must have some ultimate ground of its existence which is infinite, non-conditioned and self-subsistent, otherwise there is no sense to be made of it. That is valid enough, but why call that 'God' in the Christian meaning of the word? It can only tell us that something exists about which we are told only what it is not – i.e. that it is not-contingent. It might be the total cosmos itself, in which case 'God' would *be* the world (pantheism). Or again, there might be an omnipotent, omniscient Being who was a fiend. We can only arrive at God in the conclusion if we have already the concept of a Being, omnipotent and self-subsisting, who is absolute goodness and perfection – the God in whom Christians believe.

Moreover, as John Hick has shown, there is a further catch. The argument runs: either there is a God, or the universe remains inexplicable. But there is no logical necessity why the universe should not be inexplicable. It could be 'just there', just something that has happened, simply the resultant of blind forces, a dance of atoms in which there is no meaning. The Christian denies that this is true. But it is not an illogical position. And it is the position of many great atheists, from Lucretius to Bertrand Russell.

It follows that the choice with which we are confronted is not between faith in God and no answer at all, but between two alternative answers, incompatible with one another, which start from different presuppositions. The argument from nature to God must fail because the available evidence is ambiguous, admitting of contradictory explanations. Some aspects (beauty, order, goodness) point in a theistic direction, others (evil, suffering) in a non-theistic. The world is patient of both theistic and naturalistic interpretations. Thus 'theism is not an experimental issue. There is no test observation ... such that if A occurs theism is shown to be true, while if B occurs theism is shown to be false.'[10] Mind must take its option. The Christian option starts from faith in the rationality of the universe – for faith is what opens the door to meaning. If we opt for the theistic hypothesis, we find that it unifies and interprets ever-widening areas of our knowledge and of our experience of life, and that serves to support and reinforce the initial intuitions of faith. We can 'verify' our beliefs, but we cannot prove them. As Dr Paton wrote:

Religious principles can be confirmed only in the life of religion, just as scientific principles can be confirmed only by a successful pursuit of science. Indeed the very nature of science is such that it cannot conceivably offer any support for religion. Though a scientist may be a saint and a saint a scientist, there is no reason why we should muddle up two different kinds of outlook and expect them both to have the same kind of confirmation ... Our own good sense tells us that nothing could be more inappropriate than to judge nature by moral standards. We do not expect nature, or any part of it, to do its duty. A moral theory about the physical world as known to science, or indeed to ordinary experience, is manifest nonsense.[11]

If we cannot prove that there is a God, is not that almost fatal to the claim that what Christianity believes is true? Or may it be rather that the demand for proof misinterprets the nature of religious knowledge – and indeed, for that matter, of knowledge at all? The Greeks, as we have seen, held that true knowledge is knowledge of what is truly and fully real – the essences, the things-in-themselves. But since Descartes, and increasingly since the Enlightenment, it has been held that what we can really know – as distinct from having opinions about – is the truth of self-evident propositions; in other words, that knowledge is most certain when it conforms to the mathematical type. Thus it has come to be held that 'to know anything is equivalent to being able to prove it'.[12] Hence the preoccupation of modern philosophy with the principle of verification. I can touch on this only superficially, but the question is one of crucial importance.

How can we test whether a statement is true? Logical positivism maintained that only two kinds of statement could be true or indeed could have any real meaning – those of the mathematical type, which can be demonstrated mathematically, and those of a scientific type which can and must be empirically verified – and, in the early days of the movement, that meant by the evidence of the senses. But religious statements do not fall into either class. Religious statements, therefore, it asserted, are neither true nor false, they are simply 'meaningless'. And of course it was not only religious statements which were thus ruled out, but moral or aesthetic statements – and the verification principle itself, which can never be empirically verified and is therefore found to be self-contradictory.

Clearly this was ridiculously narrow, and it has since been virtually discarded. But philosophers still remain obsessed with the question of verification and falsification. If a statement is true, its opposite must be false. So one way of asking whether it is true is to ask what would show it to be false. If you say something about God, for instance, and maintain that what you are saying is true, you must be able to say what you would take as counting for it and what would count against it – what would have to happen to verify it and what would have to happen to falsify it. If you cannot do that, then the God you are talking about seems to suffer 'the death of a thousand qualifications' and not to be really existent at all. But that is something we never can do, for we have no unambiguous evidence. Let the reader ask himself how he would reply. (Would a rainbow verify God and an earthquake falsify him? They could both be happening at the same moment.) What, then, happens to truth in religious statements? Can they be really 'cognitive' at all? Can they be conveying any genuine knowledge about the reality of God? Or have they only a biographical interest, as statements about our own attitudes? All this has come as a shock to many believers, who fear that their faith is being undermined by radical scepticism at top levels.

As we know, some theologians have seemed to panic and rushed into self-defeating attempts to market a Christianity without God. If talk about God is so precarious, perhaps it is better to stop trying to talk about him, or to print the word in inverted commas, to show that we do not mean quite what the Bible or Christian tradition has meant in the bad old days before the arrival of logical empiricism. But what Christian thinkers ought to be doing, surely, is to challenge the philosophical assumption that the logic of scientific rationalism is the only route to genuine knowledge, or that provability is the test of truth.

For in fact we know many things that we cannot prove. For example, we know that we live in a real world, but we do not ask for proof that the world 'exists', nor, if we did, would any such proof be possible. We are perfectly certain of our own existence, although there is no possibility of proving it. We do not require a proof that they exist before we talk to our friends or kiss our wives. We just know that cruelty is wicked, though no demonstration of that can be imagined. In the same way, a man who knows, as the Bible knows, that we are in encounter with the living God, would never dream of asking to have it proved to him or be in the least more certain if it were.

There is no one paradigmatic kind of knowledge to which all genuine knowledge must conform. As Aristotle recognized long ago, there are many different kinds of knowledge, corresponding to different fields of reality. There are therefore different kinds of enquiry which require, and admit of, different kinds of evidence. Thus each line of enquiry has its own logic. The logic of mathematical demonstration, which is properly applicable to physics, cannot be applied in biology, or in ethics or the human sciences. Since God is not one object among other objects, then presumably there is some special and unique way by which he can be known. This is what religion calls faith. What Christians need to know is not that God can be proved by methods which do not and cannot apply to him, but that the religious way of knowing him – that is, faith – can be genuinely cognitive and can give us true and trustworthy knowledge, continuous though not identical with the rest of our knowledge, attained by other methods. They need to know, too, that faith is not irrational but that it can be supported by rational arguments, so that it is 'reasonable' to live by it.

In the popular mind faith means credulity – believing six impossible things before breakfast, or the schoolboy's 'believing what you know is untrue'. Admittedly some of the later scholastics tried to defend the irrational position that a statement may be accepted as true for faith while yet seen to be false by reason. But that is no part of the mainstream tradition; and it is, I should want to say, definitely sub-Christian, as sinning against the light of reason. (Statements are not in fact true 'for' anybody. Some people may think them to be true, others may reject them as untrue; but in themselves they must either be true or false. They may contain some mixture of truth and falsity. But no statement can be both true in church and false in the lecture room – it must be one thing or the other.)

Faith is not a substitute for knowledge – something with which we have to make do when no certain knowledge is to be had. Self-evidently it can never have absolute certainty – if it had, it would not be faith. But it is not a merely subjective attitude – as though it were no more than a choice of spectacles through which we prefer to view the surrounding world. Religion claims that the insights of faith are intimations of what is objectively real. Anyone's beliefs, of course, may be mistaken – there are people who firmly believe that the earth is flat; and no amount of psychological certitude, taken alone, can guarantee their validity. (It is one of the odd facts about human nature that the more plainly absurd a man's beliefs, the more obstinately he will often be found to cling to them.) Our beliefs always require objective testing. But that does not mean that faith must be a deceiver. Checked by rational and moral criticism, it is a genuine form of cognition, which may lead to a genuine knowledge of God.

Basically, perhaps, the nature of faith is something like trustful response to our environment, which is one of the conditions of being alive. Everything living is always in reaction with and response to realities outside itself. When that totally ceases we call it death; so that, as has been said, the only thing that is completely without faith is a corpse. How do the lilies of the field grow? Simply by accepting and responding to what is given to them by their environment (sun, air, soil, etc.). Jesus ascribed faith to a grain of mustard seed. In faith as a conscious activity of mind there is always, it seems, this element of givenness. Faith, in its religious connotation, is response to the sacred or 'supernatural' qualities which our total experience of the world presents to us. As the artist responds to its aesthetic qualities and the moralist to its ethical demands, so religion responds to the numinous or divine. But before we can respond to it we must recognize it. There must be some cognitive apprehension on our part.

Faith, therefore, is classed in traditional Christian usage as one of the theological virtues, since it is directed towards God, and not only, like justice, towards our fellow-men. But it is theological also, in the sense that it is a virtue divinely implanted in us and dependent on supernatural grace. For the Schoolmen, it was the God-given faculty for apprehending those revealed truths, necessary to man's eternal salvation, which are not discoverable by 'unaided' reason. The scholastic scheme of nature and supernature, or nature and grace, in a two-storey thought-world, may have no great importance for us today, any more than the finicky technical distinctions between the different kinds and degrees of grace. But the central point remains fundamentally true. Faith is dependent on grace – on God's free gift. Religion starts from God, not from man. It is born in response to the religious given – that is, to God's willed self-disclosure, for which the code-name is revelation. Faith presupposes revelation, and to some extent therefore knows God already. In Pascal's famous words, we should not be seeking for him if we had not already found him – or, better put, if he had not found us.

If God is to be made known to the minds of men, then what is revealed must be revealed *to somebody*. There cannot be revelation *in vacuo*. It cannot be just an external event that happens, like the thunderstorms round the peaks of Sinai, whether any one is aware of it or not. Nothing is transmitted if there is no reception. Nothing is revealed if nobody apprehends it. But Moses discerned a theophany in the thunderstorm and was aware of a presence among the snow-fields. There would have been no revelation of God in the decisive events of the nations's history – the exodus and the exile, for example – had not seers and prophets been 'taught by God' to interpret and acclaim them as revelatory, disclosing God in deliverance and judgment – a God of compassion and a God of righteousness.

Thus revelation in its nature is, and cannot but be, a two-way process – the given disclosure to which faith responds and the human faith that responds to it. Of both movements, manward and Godward, God is himself the source and giver. It is God, who created man in his own image, who enables him to make the response. Faith is the gift of God's 'prevenient' grace. In the human response to what is given there is, however latent and undeveloped, an activity which can rightly be called cognitive. At the level of the prophetic religion this is reflective, reasoned and elaborate and amounts to what I have called interpretation. But even in primitive religious experience this factor can never be entirely lacking. Religion no doubt moves at deeper levels and satisfies deeper needs of the psyche than conscious intellectual reasoning. It appeals to – some would say, arises from – the depths of the uncharted unconscious. It is clear from such knowledge as we possess that the religion of primitive societies is primarily non-rational and emotional – an almost instinctive or reflex reaction to the uncanny, the mysterious *numen*. Confrontation with the awesome feels dangerous and may sometimes frighten people half out of their lives. It can have purely physical accompaniments – the goose-flesh, the cold shiver down the spine. But it is an awareness of confrontation by a power or presence other than the self. And the point to make here is that it is recognized as a distinctive and special form of experience which differs in kind from all other forms. However undeveloped and undefined, it is, even at that stage, cognition. There seems to be no response from the human side – even the cry 'How dreadful is this place' – which does not contain an intellectual element, some potential activity of the thinking mind. If that is not true, it is difficult to see how the higher religions could ever have developed out of their primitive, elementary origins. From the moment that man has been in possession of language, he has the power to form and communicate concepts.

In traditional Christian thinking, revelation has been held to be attested by miracle. Miraculous signs and wonders were taken as evidence of God's activity in self-disclosure, or as 'proving the divinity of Christ'. Thus miracles were an aid to faith. In the different thought-world in which we live, a great deal of evidence is required before we are able to believe in miracles –

and this, I should want to add, is as it should be; credulity is not a Christian virtue. Could there be a non-miraculous Christianity? It could at a pinch probably go on even if it had to discard miracle, at least in its popular conventional meaning. What it cannot dispense with is revelation. There can be no non-supernatural Christianity. The question is how far the miracle stories strengthen the case for divine revelation. Are they really evidence for belief in God? In the past – or so it now seems to us – the emphasis has been thrown on the wrong place, on the abnormality or inexplicability of the alleged miraculous events. But events are not divine because they are odd or because we can find no alternative explanation of them, like the acts of God in an insurance policy. They could be due to witchcraft or black magic ('He casts out devils by Beelzebub'). Or there may be perfectly natural explanations as the gaps close in our scientific knowledge. It is not their oddity or abnormality which makes them truly disclosure situations, truly revelations of God, but their moral and religious content, assessed – for us – in the light of Christ himself.

This principle applies over the whole field. How can we tell whether any alleged revelation really is a revelation of God and therefore genuinely deserving credence, not merely hallucinatory or even faked? First, by careful scrutiny of the evidence and the reliability of the witnesses by all the revelant canons of criticism; and then, surely, by rational reflection on its ethical and religious content and – if we are Christians – its compatibility with what we know about God through Jesus Christ. Nothing can be true about God which contradicts his teaching and his character. As Leonard Hodgson used to insist so often, 'Content is the criterion of source'.

It is by such means that faith can be 'verified'. As Hick remarks in the book from which I have quoted, to verify is a transitive verb. Verification is something that we do, not something that happens to propositions. We shall have verified any statement either by removing rational grounds for doubting it, or by having satisfied ourselves that there are sufficient rational grounds for believing it. Here faith and reason are met together.

Uncertainty, of course, still remains. Faith cannot wait on absolute demonstration; and (as we have seen) statements of fact – e.g. that Jesus was raised from the dead – are in their nature incapable of proof. Faith is always partly a matter of will. We have always to decide between alternatives, to choose to which side we will direct belief and to which we will commit ourselves for life and death. In all our choices, not only in religion, probability is the guide of life. And as Joseph Butler said, 'in matters of great moment', such as our religious and ethical decisions, we are under obligation to decide for what we deliberately judge to have the support of the highest probability. Honest religion must take an enormous risk and must always have the courage to doubt, which is integral to faith and implied in it. But there is no room for a non-committal attitude – to decide for that is already a decision. Faith in its full religious meaning is an existential decision, involving the commitment of the total self.

Is it true?

There is in the end only one reason for the acceptance of Christianity – that we believe Christianity is true. Can we say that – and what should we mean by saying it? There is the ultimate, life and death question, which we have now honestly to face. In the last two sections we have been preparing for it. We have seen that in spite of the now prevailing relativism the question of truth does still arise. We have seen that faith and reason are not opposed, and that there can be reasonable grounds for faith. We have seen, moreover, that faith as believing *in* implies believing *that* certain things which we believe about somebody are true. Fundamentally, faith (as I tried to suggest) is trust – and trust in something not yet apparent or visible. Faith in its famous scriptural definition is 'what makes us certain of realities we do not see' (Heb. 11.1 NEB). Christian faith is trust in God and Jesus Christ, not only believing things about them. A man could, for example, believe that all the reported miracles did happen and that Jesus really was born of a virgin, and yet not believe in him in the Christian sense. But that faith, that trust, involves believing that certain statements about him are true, and without that belief it could not exist. The two are inseparably interlocked. Trust, of course, can be disappointed; the hero may fail in the hour of crisis. Thus faith and doubt are not mutually exclusive; faith must always fall short of demonstrability. Religious faith is essentially the trust that the God in whom it believes will not fail. To believe that Christianity is true might be said to mean to believe that the God in whom Christians trust is the real God and that he is truly revealed in Jesus Christ. And that implies believing in the truth of the fundamental Christian affirmations.[13]

But here we run into the million-dollar question. What is meant by truth in religious statements? This is the nerve-centre of the whole debate about the truth of the Christian religion. We have already glanced at some of the difficulties created by current fashions in philosophy. But it is not only a twentieth-century problem. It is and always has been inherent in any attempt to speak about God at all. The creature cannot know what it is to be God. We are like Plato's prisoners in a cave, who can see only the shadows cast on the wall by the sun which they cannot directly perceive. We cannot look straight into the sun, it blinds us. No man, said the Hebrews, can see God and live. But if human thought cannot contain God, how can he be spoken of in human language, and how can it be claimed that any such language is true? It is clear that it cannot be true in the same sense as the language we use about empirical objects. So we are always exposed to the charge of double-think, of saying one thing when we really mean something else. Why cannot Christians say what they really do mean?

On the popular level, most of the objections, so far as they rest on reasoned grounds at all, are due to the mis-understanding of Christian language – taking the words of Christian creeds and liturgies as though they were meant as literal descriptions of the being of God, which is what they never can be. The conviction which lies at the heart of Christianity is that the deepest truth about God cannot be spoken in words; it can only be lived, and has been lived in Jesus the

Christ. The Fourth Gospel sometimes speaks about *doing* the truth; and Barth coined a phrase that is often quoted – Christ is the knowability of God.

Those who have been most deeply aware of God have always felt the pressure of this constraint, due to the limitations of human speech – all, that is to say, except One, who apparently felt no such inhibitions and spoke of him confidently and directly with the authority of immediate knowledge. This compunction is plainly evident, for instance, in such a profound theologian as Augustine, who wrote twenty-two books *On the Trinity*, 'not in order that this should be said, but in order not to say nothing'. Some great thinkers have chosen the latter alternative. Whatever we say about God, they have insisted, must be so inadequate, so far from the whole truth, as to be misleading or positively false. That can be avoided only by keeping silence. The negative way is the only way of safety. John Scotus Erigena said that God is Nothing. The mystics, in all religions, have wished to go beyond all verbal statements and all differentiations of thought to be united with the absolute One. (The uncharacterized, all-absorbing One – or the All – is not far from the Nothing.) But if nothing whatever can rightly be said about God, then religion remains for ever incommunicable, and believers cannot tell even themselves what they believe or on what their faith is grounded. That would seem to end in a kind of religious nihilism.

If we speak about God it can be only indirectly and analogically. That is possible because there is something, at least, which can be said both about God and man. There is something, at least, which they have in common. God and man, for example, both exist. If God created man in his own image, there is a certain analogy of being, and the predicates which we apply to man may be applied, so far as they can take us – which can never be the whole way – to God. Human experience and human knowledge can thus be intimations of God's reality, analogies by which we can make statements which, though they cannot convey the whole truth, may nevertheless be true so far as they go. We can speak, for example, about the wisdom of God, on the analogy of human wisdom. There must be wisdom in God in some eminent way; but it must so far tran-scend human wisdom that, if taken as an actual account, what we say can be to that extent untrue.

The meaning of analogy is proportion: A is to B as C is to D. Reason is to the soul as the eye to the body. They are not the same thing, but it is possible to predicate the same thing of both; what they have in common is that they both illuminate. Yet even in saying that, we are attempting to use the language of physical causation as though it applied to the immaterial mind. If pressed too far, to its logical conclusion, any and every analogy breaks down. It can take us only to a certain point, and however far, no nearer to infinity. But unless we do go that far, by some such method, we are all condemned to complete re-ligious aphasia, and the Trappist will be the only authentic Christian.

As many readers of this will know, Karl Barth vehemently and radically rejected the whole notion of an analogy of being – and with it, all natural theology. There is, he insisted, no way from man to God. No human thought or insight can lay a track. God's own Word is the sole source of knowledge. Thereby in effect he cut Christianity off from the field of any rational discussion with people who want to think about their religion. That was why his pupil Bonhoeffer broke with him and con-demned dialectical theology as no more than a 'positivism of revelation' – an unsupported take-it-or-leave-it dogmatism.

The uses of analogy were worked out in great detail and elaboration by the philosophers of the Middle Ages, and their findings persist in Thomist theology. The more recent way of meeting the same point is the recognition that religious language is essentially, and inevitably must be, symbolic rather than literally descriptive. Does this imply that 'It's only a lot of fairy tales'? The apostles dismissed the reports of the Marys on the first Easter Day as 'idle tales' – the sort of thing that overstrained women would say, symptoms of their neurotic condition but not accounts of an actual event. Words, words, words – are they nothing more than that, smoke-screens to conceal the emptiness of the heavens?

Words are devised as tools of communication and their

meaning is to be looked for in their usage. It is people who mean things by the words they use, not words that decide what people mean. The way people use words, the way they talk, depends on the kind of people they are, their mental habits and cultural situations. So in course of time words change their meanings. The Prayer Book bids us to pray that the magistrates may truly and indifferently (impartially) minister justice, which to us now suggests making a poor job of it. Where vocabulary is undeveloped, one word may have to be used in more than one sense (as it often is in the Greek New Testament), or it may have different meanings in different contexts, or may mean different things to different people. Confusion and mis-understanding often arise when the parties engaged in a debate use the same word with different connotations.[14] It is too often assumed that religious sentences, because they are built up with the same words and in the same grammatical form, mean the same thing as scientific sentences – in which case they can be written off as nonsense. What is the significance of religious language?

'There's a Friend for little children above the bright blue sky.' Is it true, Mummy?

How ought that question to be answered? If the verse is taken as literal description, the straight and truthful answer is No: there is nobody sitting up there above the clouds. But to give it will help to create a hardened sceptic, disillusioned at a tender age and immunized against religious teaching. If elabor-ate explanations are attempted they suggest that Mum does not believe it either. The harassed parent tends to fall back on, 'Hush, dear, you mustn't be irreverent'. That hymn is now de-rided by the experts who theorize about child-psychology. But how better present to the imagination the Christian experience of trust – that our lives are in the hand of a God who 'never faileth, whose love will never die'? As the shades of the prison house begin to close and the child discovers how much life can hurt him, he will suspect that he has been deceived, that this was just kid-stuff that his parents taught him, and the Great Friend will dissolve like Santa Claus. But if he grows up under favourable conditions – a secure home and enlightened Christian teaching – he may come to learn that neither life nor death can separate us from the love of God, and that the hymn was true after all. When he is an old man he will rejoice in it. But the meaning of truth here seems to be equivocal. The hymn is true in one sense and not in another. Truth seems to be used in two different senses. Is such a procedure honest, or defensible? Can there be more than one kind of truth?

'I believe in one Lord, Jesus Christ, the only begotten Son God . . . who for us men and for our salvation came down from heaven and was incarnate by the Holy Ghost of the Virgin Mary and was made man.' Millions of Christians in all times and places have built their lives on that great affirmation. But is it true? Or ought it to be discarded? And if so, what becomes of Christianity? Here again we seem to be caught in the same dilemma. For as literal description this is not true. Jesus did not 'descend' from the stratosphere, any more than he is physically seated by the throne of God in a super-terrestrial palace. But will any Christian say that it is 'untrue'? That would be to deny the deepest intuitions and experience of the universal church.

The point here is that a factual description conveys truth at the elementary level at which it can be tested empirically, by sight, touch, measurement and so forth, or tested against other incidents of the same kind. But factual description is not by any means the only way in which truth can be communicated. It can be stated, for instance, through the fine arts. So too it can be communicated through poetry, through drama and fiction. If truth cannot be conveyed through fiction, what are we going to say about the parables?

To take a perhaps rather hackneyed poem, Shelley's 'Ode to a Skylark' begins:

> Hail to thee, blithe spirit,
> Bird thou never wert.

As a plain factual statement this is absurd. If the creature was not a bird, then it obviously cannot have been a skylark. Yet the poet's vision discovers something which could not be apparent to an ornithologist, classifying it by genus and species. Thus the invocation does convey truth – as we sometimes say, a deeper truth about it. We need to recall the insights of Coleridge about the uses of imagination – as distinct from mere fancy – in apprehending reality. A statement that is not factually true may yet be a way of communicating truth.

Is Hamlet true? The incidents presented in it had not ever occurred in 'real life'. Wherever Shakespeare found the original plot, the incidents belong to the 'world' of the play – an imaginary world which he constructed, and in which, while it lasts, the audience have to live. But no sane man would call Hamlet 'untrue'. Here we have truth conveyed through dramatic action. It tells us truth about life itself, truth about the human situation. The same can be claimed for any great novel, which can be said, in a rather weary phrase, to be 'an exploration in depth' of something that is true about human character. Thus truth seems to exist, as it were, on two planes. There is truth of literal description and truth of interpretation or understanding.

What, to go a bit further, is the answer to the stock question, Is the Bible true? Is it merely a matter of straight factual accuracy? Did the walls of Jericho really fall down? And if they did not, would that 'disprove' the Bible? It is sometimes claimed that what has been unearthed on some of the biblical sites by the archaeologists has triumphantly vindicated its truth. All they have really done is to make it clear that the historical parts of the Old Testament are more historical than had been supposed. (Much of it is poetry and drama and had never even pretended to be factual.) But they leave untouched the truth of the Bible in any sense that matters to religion, as saving truth about God – all that we mean when we call it the Word of God. Or again, New Testament scholarship now inclines to the view that the Fourth Gospel is closer to early Palestinian sources and as sheer narrative may be more reliable than pre-war liberalism had allowed for. That is reassuring, so far as it goes. But the truth of St John's writing is not there. 'These things were written,' says the author, 'that ye might believe that Jesus is the Christ, the Son of God, and that believing ye may have life through his name.' The real question is whether *that* is true.

It may be a hazardous thing to say, but it almost looks as though truth were multi-form or, at any rate, multi-dimensional. What do we mean by truth in a work of art? In one usage, we mean aesthetic truth. Anyone can see that the Albert Memorial or the Peter Pan figure are fake, are false and bogus, while Westminster Abbey or such a statue as Michelangelo's David are true. But this is a matter of aesthetic values, not one of accuracy in representation; you can have that, yet a thoroughly trivial figure. The artist's vision, we judge, has been myopic; he has not been able to see into the heart of things, and so he has been putting us off with a half-truth.

Or consider the difference between a Titian portrait and a snapshot. The latter reproduces empirical facts, the former reveals 'more than meets the eye' and discloses truth about the man himself which may be a surprise even to the sitter. He may protest that he does not look like that, but it may be a true interpretation of him. (When a portrait of Archbishop Lang was commissioned the artist asked. 'Which archbishop am I to paint?') What I am suggesting is that when we ask whether Christianity is true, it is truth of this kind about which we are enquiring.

Factual truth can be stated in straight prose; transcendental or metaphysical truth, only by means of imagery or symbol, in language which is not literally descriptive but indirect, allusive and evocative, pointing to meta-empirical realities which out-range the categories of space and time.

The simplest illustration of this is the metaphorical language of the Bible. Metaphor takes us beyond empirical fact and throws new light on a total situation. It is not merely a stylish way of saying something that could equally well be said in straight prose. It opens a window into a truth deeper than can be conveyed through plain words, and may therefore be claimed as a genuine form of cognition. We may say of a man that he is a lion, a snake in the grass, a wee timorous beastie. He is none of these things, he is a man. Yet it tells us more and tells it more vividly than can be learnt from the commonplace statement that he is brave or treacherous or fearful. Metaphor quickens the imagination by the association of words and images, which is the proper business of poetry, and thus enables us to see something which we cannot or do not see with the bodily eye.

For metaphor is the language of vision. What it is, in its actual usage, is a comparison, suggesting that something is like something else and thereby throwing more light on what it is. The scientist, seeking to give an account of anything, analyses it into its component parts or classifies it under some general law. The poet and artist see it in a vision, in its wholeness, as the unique thing it is. But because it is a unique thing, that vision can only be conveyed by a comparison, by telling us what that unique thing is 'like'. The metaphor helps us to see what he has seen by his own divination or intuition.

This is the method of Jesus in many parables – a method which, he said, he had to employ because the multitudes 'seeing did not see and hearing did not understand.' In our attempts to interpret the parables we have to be clear just what is the point of comparison. 'The kingdom of heaven is like' – and there follows a story. If we treat the story as an allegory, in which every detail has a 'heavenly meaning', we can easily reach a quite false conclusion – if, for example, God is meant to be indicated by the lord who commended the unjust steward. Take the treasure hidden in the field. The peasant who found it was rather doubtfully honest: he buried the treasure under the soil again and bought the field as agricultural land. The point of comparison is that, like the treasure, the kingdom can only be had at the price of all we possess. But once we know that the kingdom is 'like' that, we know more about what it is and what it means for us.

Everything, or at any rate every living thing, is unique, the thing it is and nothing else. Yet it has some qualities in common with other things, and accordingly some illuminating comparison can be made. God is unique totally and absolutely, and not in a class with any other realities. Thus, strictly speaking, there can be no comparisons. 'To whom will ye liken me?' says the Lord. Metaphors, like analogies, break down, and can only be used just so far as they will go. Yet we have to use them; we have no other instrument. All the biblical writers use metaphor when they speak of the God of whom we cannot speak. He is Shepherd, Father, Husband, King, Lawgiver, a rock of defence, a consuming fire. None of these, obviously, are literal truth. How much harm has been done, for example, by thinking of God as literally Lawgiver? But they can and do indicate genuine truth about God as known in religious experience. The great metaphors in the Fourth Gospel – the Good Shepherd, the Light of the World, the Bread of Life, the Vine – which are there attributed to the Lord himself, tell us more about what he means to the believer than any number of articles in a dictionary.[15]

It is, no doubt, in the nature of metaphor that, through failure in knowledge, understanding or insight, it can be false, inadequate or misleading and so end by hiding rather than illuminating the reality towards which it is meant to point. This is so, notoriously, in religious metaphors. But, as most people apparently think in pictures, false metaphors can create false images; and to worship a false image is idolatry. Then is the time when 'our image of God must go'. Clearly, all the time all our images have to be continually revised and criticized – that is how we grow in the knowledge of God. There is no infallible prescription for discerning true metaphors from false. It can only be done by comparing them with our other knowledge and by moral and rational reflection; and that is part of the job of the theologian.

Metaphors may be built up into similes, and these are the peaks in some of the greatest poetry: in Homer and Virgil, in Dante and Milton.

Dante thought of light as a symbol of the spiritual life, and in his great poem he describes, accurately and economically, light in its varying effects – the light of dawn, light on the sea, the light on leaves in spring. But all these beautiful descriptions, which are the part of Dante that many of us like best, are similes: they are introduced by the words 'as when'. *They are intended only to illustrate and make comprehensible to our earth-bound senses a vision of divine order and heavenly beauty.*[16]

Or similes can be further built up and elaborated into an allegory or story, a fictitious narrative like *Pilgrim's Progress*, which incomparably communicates truth about the soul's relation to God. The most ancient form of fictitious narrative conveying truth can be seen in the great myths. To the popular mind myth suggests 'mere legend', and simple Christians are shocked when theologians talk about 'the myth of Christianity'. But a myth is a story which is not merely legendary but conveys in an imaginary form profound interpretations of human experiences. Psychologists are throwing much new light on this. Anthony Storr, for example, has pointed out how deeply true is the story of Little Red Riding Hood.[17] The wolf is found in Granny's bed; the wolf and Granny are the same person. An over-possessive Granny or Mum may be a devourer who destroys us. So the hero and giant-killer myths, imaginary though they are in form – for these things never actually happened – convey truth about the journey to adulthood.

Religion always generates myths: creation myths, redemption myths and so forth. Nearly all have myths or stories of the hero in the experiences and adventures involved in his being the saviour and deliverer, and by which his saviourhood was achieved. Christianity has from the first found expression in the great Christian myth – the old, old story – of one who for love of men and for our salvation came down from heaven and took our nature upon him and suffered and died for us and rose from the dead and opened the gate of everlasting life. The gospel of God is proclaimed in that story, not in a set of abstract propositions – not only the story in the gospels but the whole story that Christianity tells, of how God so loved the world that he gave his only begotten Son. Some are asking, 'Cannot we now dispense with it?' One of those who have recently asked that adds, 'Would that mean a different religion?'

It is now a recognized principle in the study of early forms of religion that 'the thing done' comes before 'the word spoken'; the ritual is prior to the myth, worship is prior to the theology which then grows up to interpret and inform it. Worship is the language of religion. The real meaning of religious words –

what Christians mean by them when we use them – must be sought in the experience of worship, where we *know* what we try to verbalize in speech. Can we say that a religious myth is true myth if it evokes and strengthens in the worshipper that faith in God and that Christian experience out of which it was originally born?

Religious language is the attempt to speak about infinite and non-spatial reality. But human minds are conditioned by space-time, and therefore we can speak only in spatial metaphor – in terms of what Bultmann calls 'objectifying' – which can do no more than hint at divine reality and, if taken too literally, may be false. We are obliged to use words which apply to our ordinary experience as 'models', for there are no other words for us to use – and then we have to proceed at once to 'qualify' them, lest they should become positively misleading.[18] Thus we speak of Christ as the Son of God, but we add words like only or only-begotten to make clear that we do not mean Son in exactly the same sense in which he was son of David or son of Mary. (Origen spoke of 'eternal generation'.)

If he cannot know the infinite God through our logic, the rules of thought for our finite minds, there will always be something logically 'odd' in any attempt to speak about him at all. We are always exposed to attack by philosophy, because the Infinite cannot be contained in any finite system of thought, and religious language must always seem to it to be self-contradictory and unverifiable. This 'logical oddity' is reflected, inevitably, in religious language, in the 'odd' way in which words have to be used. There is never a one-to-one correspondence between the words and that to which they refer. They can be no more than symbolic, allusive, pointers but never literally descriptive. Does this mean that they cannot communicate genuine knowledge?

If it is, and must be, essentially symbolic, how can we claim that religious language is true? For the claim that Christianity is true must mean that Christians are telling the truth in what they say about God and Jesus Christ. We may reject propositional revelation, and insist that God is revealed in a person.

But as John Hick says, that does not mean that no propositions can be framed about what has thus been revealed. In effect, the creeds are those propositions. The creeds are declarations of faith: I believe in God, and in Jesus Christ, and in the Holy Spirit. But they also declare that this trust has actual content, that it implies believing certain things about them. The creeds are not only personal commitments; they are also stating that something is the case. God is maker of heaven and earth, Jesus Christ is his only Son, our Lord, who was crucified 'for us', and so on. The fundamental Christian affirmations are interpretations, in words never fully adequate, of what Christian faith and experience have found in the Lord's life and death and resurrection – that this is true God and eternal life. They are true if that experience is authentic and if our God is the real God. Do we think that an impersonal abstraction, which can be tidily packed in our logic, is more real than the living God of persons, the Father of our Lord Jesus Christ?

Logically, writes Professor Baelz,

There is a gap between religious belief and other forms of belief. It is like coming to realize the Presence of something which has been present all the time, but to the existence of which we have been blind. It is not a new experience to be set alongside other kinds of experience. It embraces and illuminates all other experience. The religious 'object', correspondingly, is seen as the Ground of all other objects. It is 'the transcendent in the midst'.[19]

Nobody can prove the truth of Christianity. Nobody can do more for the enquirer than to point him to the full available evidence and to show him that there are reasonable grounds, indeed grounds of the highest probability, for believing what it says and what it stands for. Then he has to make his own choice and nobody else can make the decision for him. The decisive evidence is experimental. At the end of the day no man can decide whether Christian beliefs are true beliefs simply and solely as the result of argument – though argument may have an important function as a *preparatio evangelica*, and the church should be better equipped to present it. He can decide only by trying to live by them, in self-committal to Christ as Lord and Saviour.

Lord, to whom shall we go? Come and see.

NOTES

1. Peter Berger, *A Rumour of Angels*, p. 47.

2. Alasdair MacIntyre, *Secularization and Moral Change*, Oxford University Press, 1967, p. 12.

3. J. Bronowski, *The Identity of Man*, Heinemann, 1966, p. 12.

4. Peter Berger, op. cit., pp. 57, 59.

5. H. J. Paton, *The Modern Predicament*, Allen and Unwin, 1955, p. 367.

6. Peter Baelz, *Theology and Metaphysics*, Epworth Press, 1968, p. 108.

7. In mediaeval language, schools means universities, originating in the schools of Paris. Thus school theology is that of the critical intellect, in contrast with the traditionalism of monastic teaching, e.g. at Cluny. Hence the clash between Bernard and Abelard. The schoolmen were not sunk in dogmatic slumbers and superstitions, as moderns who know no history imagine.

8. Natural, i.e. rational, what the mind of man can discover for itself, by contrast with revealed theology.

9. The proofs are discussed by John Hick in *Faith and Knowledge*, Macmillan,[2] 1967, and in H. J. Paton's Gifford lectures, *The Modern Predicament* (see above). Professor Hick uses the same material in his paperback *The Existence of God*, Macmillan, 1963, where the relevant documents are printed. There is an admirable discussion of the ontological proof there on pp. 3ff., 23ff.

10. John Hick, *Faith and Knowledge*, p. 145.

11. Paton, op. cit., pp. 360, 366.

12. For this paragraph see Hick, *Faith and Knowledge*, pp. 3–17.

13. There are echoes here of Wolfhart Pannenberg, *The Apostles Creed*, SCM Press, 1972, p. 6: 'Believing trust cannot be separated from the trusting person's belief in the truth of the thing in which he trusts and towards which his trust is directed.'

14. Compare 'faith' in St Paul and St James.

15. For the last few paragraphs see Austin Farrer, *Reflective Faith*, SPCK, 1972, pp. 24–38. He there remarks: 'But please don't think

I'm going to tell you that theology is just figurative poetry; that is a very wicked thing to say, though some people have not shrunk from it.'

16. Clark, *Civilisation*, pp. 85f. Italics mine.

17. Anthony Storr, *On Human Aggression*, Penguin Books, 1971, pp. 39ff.

18. See Ian T. Ramsey, *Religious Language*, SCM Press, 1957, ch. 1.

19. Baelz, op. cit., p. 109.

4 | Freedom and permissiveness

But, the crucial test of the truth of Christian doctrine is the validity of the Christian ethic. The two are, of course, inseparably connected. What is distinctively Christian in Western ethics rests on the Christian beliefs about God and man. No doubt the broad-minded thing to say now is that one can no longer accept the Christian doctrines but certainly wishes to retain the Christian ethic; and for most people today 'Christianity' means a particular kind of behaviour rather than a particular kind of belief. But if the beliefs underlying it are false, the case for Christian morality collapses. If it is not the truth, it cannot be the way. (The suggestion sometimes made by secular humanism that the ethical teaching of Jesus remains valid although his religious beliefs were mistaken, violates all psychological probability as well as all the evidence of the gospels, which record no 'purely ethical' teaching which is separable from his religion. Every word he spoke and every thing he did issued out of his knowledge of God. If he was wrong at the centre of his thinking, how can he be trusted as a guide to life? A delusion cannot inspire a true way of living.)

Conversely, if the Christian beliefs generate a morality that is false, the pragmatic argument for their truth breaks down: they must be not only false but injurious, and the sooner they are discarded the better. Either way, belief and practice are inseparable. It is no new thing for Christian beliefs to be criticized or rejected on moral grounds. For example, some of the nineteenth-century free-thinkers passionately attacked the doctrine of the atonement – as that was taught by Victorian

Protestantism – as being 'in the highest degree unethical'; and theology needs constant purification, from within and without, by moral criticism. But by and large, Christian morality has been the basis of Western civilization, and still persists in secularized form. Constitutionally ours is a Christian country, and broadly speaking the Christian law commands a general consensus among the people. (Self-evidently, in a pluralist and increasingly multi-racial and multi-religious society such as ours, not all citizens call themselves Christians or regard Christian standards as binding on them. But they do not say they are actually immoral.)

What is new is that the Christian ethic should be criticized and rejected as false morality. Always from the first the average sensual man has been in rebellion against the Christian ethic because it made such exacting demands upon him, but he has hitherto paid it lip-service (if only the tribute that vice pays to virtue, i.e. by being a proper Christian hypocrite). But there is now an organized pressure-group working to extirpate the Christian ethic and to bring it into contempt as a bad ethic which does violence to human nature – anti-humanistic and repressive and a road-block holding up the march to freedom. If they succeed in capturing public opinion, Christian beliefs will be more and more discredited and before long Christian civilization will have gone down, and human values with it. So what is at stake is more than our Christianity; it is man himself in his human dignity; and the Christian faith, not for the first time, stands in the world as the champion of man.

If we want to see Christian values re-established – if we want to serve and succour our fellow-men in their attempts to vindicate their humanity against the cyclonic force of new movements which nobody really understands – we must be prepared to state a convincing case for them. It is totally useless to be merely shocked and go on denouncing the wickedness of the world or 'bleating fatuously about love' (William Temple) like so many hippies or drop-outs from society. It is no good offering facile 'Christian answers' – there are no ready-made Christian answers – or repeating conventional Christian moral judgments, for some of these may be themselves sub-

Christian. We must meet the attack at a far deeper level. Nothing we say will carry much conviction if it does not come to terms with the real problem, both in the facts of the moral situation and in the difficulties which are raised by the prevailing trends in moral philosophy – and (as we have seen already) epistemology.

The churches appear to be singularly unable to make a convincing statement of their own case, which is being allowed too often to go by default. Christians themselves are bewildered and confused in the cross-currents to which they are now exposed – men cannot bear too much change too fast – and here as elsewhere show signs of losing their nerve. The best way of restoring Christian confidence is to offer help with some fundamental thinking about some of the basic questions involved in the very nature of morality – for before we can discuss Christian ethics we must know where we stand about ethics in itself. That is what I am setting out to do in this chapter, even though in some places it may be heavy going. We are not all required to be professors; but we shall remain at the mercy of specious argument if we are not prepared to do our homework.

Freedom

'Nothing is true and everything is permitted.' There we have the logical conclusion of all-out relativism in thought and morals. It is, said Nietzsche, what is bound to happen when men have killed God and 'God is dead', and man has hoisted himself on the vacant throne. But, as Nietzsche himself so tragically realized, the end of that road is inevitably nihilism. Is that where Western society is heading? The revolt against an 'authoritarian' ethic, and indeed the rejection of all absolute values, springs out of that relativistic scepticism – inability to believe in anything ultimate – which is endemic in the air we breathe. It presents itself in the name of freedom. Is it a genuine step on the way to freedom and the vindication of human responsibility – for if it is, Christians would have to welcome it – or does it threaten to rob of us our humanness and enslave us

65

again in the anarchy of the dark ages? (Nietzsche himself remarked, it may be remembered, that it spelt the abdication of human dignity.) How is freedom related to 'permissiveness'?

To answer that we must look more closely at freedom. What is it? Is freedom merely absence of restraint, or is it an interior condition which can be preserved even in captivity? Is it something that belongs to man 'by nature', but taken from him or restricted by the 'artificial conventions' of society? (Nothing human is ever purely 'natural'. The state of nature in that sense never existed.) 'Liberty,' declared John Stuart Mill in the high summer of English utilitarianism, 'consists in doing what one desires.' Yet, whether from choice or necessity, most of us spend a great deal of our time doing things that we do not desire to do (washing up or catching the commuter train), which, whether we like it or not, just have to be done. Is that incompatible with freedom? Or can we be free in freely deciding to do them? Some of us may be impelled by a sense of duty to do what we strongly desire not to do, which is contrary to our inclinations; and we know that if we accept a moral standard there are things which we shall no longer be free to do. But what does that mean? There is nothing to stop our doing them except some strange interior necessity. Is that a violation of freedom? Is there a radical incompatibility between freedom and moral obligation?

Freedom, in the Christian understanding of it, is primarily moral and religious – freedom for something, not only from something; freedom to realize our true nature, to become what God wills us to be. Jesus himself has sometimes been described as the one perfectly free man. Yet the core of his life was filial obedience; he was free in his dependence on God; and that life is the paradigm of Christian freedom.

No one who reads the Bible can doubt for a moment that God wills man to be free, without and within. The foundation of the biblical faith in God is the deliverance out of the house of bondage. 'Thus says the Lord: Let my people go.' In that escape of a gang of fugitive slaves, Israel saw the hand of the living God leading man towards his divine destiny. Freedom is written all over the New Testament and is integral to the Chris-

66

tian gospel. Where the Spirit of the Lord is, there is liberty; and wherever the name of Christ has been proclaimed, it has brought a new sense of human dignity, new demands for freedom and emancipation. Men must be free because all human persons are of equal value in the eyes of God, and in Christ all humanity has been ennobled. Under God, freedom is part of man's birthright. (This is not the same thing as saying that 'Man is born free' – which has a political slant.) In the Christianized West it is generally accepted that human rights include the four freedoms. The American founding fathers declared that man has an inalienable right to life, liberty and the pursuit of happiness. The source of that was the theory of natural law and John Locke's political philosophy. But it would not have seemed 'self-evident' to Jefferson without the Christian tradition behind him. In the classical world it would have seemed pure nonsense. The ancient culture rested on slavery, and even so great a philosopher as Aristotle maintained that some men are by nature slaves.[1]

But short of actual slavery, men are not free if their lives and liberties are at the mercy of social anarchy and naked force, or of exploitation by powerful interests. It used to be thought that freedom would best be served by a weak state and a minimum of 'interference'. But *laissez-faire* did not make for freedom, except for the stronger to exploit the weaker. Under present conditions the state must be strong enough to control the competing organized power-groups and maintain at least some measure of equal justice. Pure individualism is no answer. But without authority there can be no justice. Civic freedom requires the reign of law – it is what the English have always believed and stood for.

But this in itself does not make a free man. A slave may be set free in his legal status but yet retain a servile mentality. The slaves who escaped across the Red Sea were always wanting to go back to Egypt, to the melons and cucumbers in the house of bondage. 'Liberty,' said G. B. Shaw, 'means responsibility; that is why most men dread it.' We have to be inwardly set free for freedom; and that is the freedom proclaimed by the gospel. When St Paul boasted, 'But I was born free', he meant that he

67

was by birth a Roman citizen, while Claudius Lysias had to buy his franchise (Acts 22.28). He had all the legal securities of freedom, yet he knew that he was a slave 'sold under sin': he was not inwardly a free man, nor free to obey the law of God. He could not just say 'I will obey' and do it; he was not free to make that decision, though no outward restrictions prevented him from making it. We are all sadly familiar with that condition. Our wills are divided against themselves and we are not free to will what God wills for us. The liberty with which Christ has set us free is the 'freedom which liberates man even from himself for his own true self, because it has its foundation outside ourselves (*extra nos*) in God and in his revelation through Jesus Christ ... Freedom is founded on the divine reality fore-given to men, which has first of all to free men for freedom.'[2]

That is the freedom of the Christian man: freedom for the fulfilment of his humanness, in responsibility before God and within the framework of moral law, summarized in the Great Commandments. Christian freedom is not antinomianism. It is the exact opposite of licence. 'If you would enter into life (authentic living)', Jesus himself said, 'keep the commandments.' The notion of freedom now being offered us, labelled with the cant word permissiveness, is in truth the antithesis of freedom as understood in the Christian tradition.

There is nothing wrong with permissiveness in itself. When it means, as in popular usage it now does, the repudiation of all norms of conduct, it is then that it becomes incompatible either with Christianity or with freedom. In the popular press and the entertainment industry, permissiveness has come to be identified with totally unrestrained sexuality. The question, How permissive can you get? means in practice, How far can you go with indecent exposure and get away with it? Sex is torn out of its personal context and presented as merely physical gratification. (The worst thing that can happen to a boy or girl is assumed to be failure to achieve an orgasm.) But 'free' sex, on such terms, is no more free than unrestrained indulgence in meths or drugs: it becomes addictive. It is surrender to physical compulsion. And the man who surrenders himself to his passions is not a free man at all; he is a slave. Permissiveness, in its present connotation, is the contradictory of moral freedom.

Metaphysical freedom

But is the whole notion of freedom illusory? Is the will really free at all? Are we not all inexorably involved in such a nexus of causal determinism that no action could have been other than it was? For if so, it is useless to talk about morality. Metaphysical freedom is the presupposition of any discussion of moral obligation. If we are not free, we are not moral agents, for the things we do are just happenings, not actions, merely 'behaviour' to be observed externally like the behaviour of sub-human species, but in no sense proceeding from within or expressions of genuine intentionality. Unless we are, within certain limits, responsible for our choices and decisions, then attribution of praise or blame is meaningless, and words like right and wrong are devoid of content. (We cannot describe an earthquake as cruel or say that the wolf 'ought not' to have killed the sheep.) All human moral experience, and even the ordinary use of language, takes 'freedom of the will' for granted. But is that a gigantic racial illusion — a belief in freedom which is itself determined, or one of those tricks that nature plays on us to prevent the species from dying out?

Christians know that the will is not free — not because we are externally determined but because of that inner self-contradiction which in religious language is called sin. But that is not the same thing as determinism in the sense in which it is opposed to 'free will'. It is this latter with which we are now concerned.

'Before we had our philosophy lectures,' remarked an innocent student, 'I never realized that there is really no such thing as freedom.' I forbear to comment on the sidelight which that remark throws on some of the goings-on in higher education in this country. 'Before we had our philosophy lectures' — what kind of lectures, I wonder, can they have had? Were they given by some half-baked sociologist, too much the slave of the new

69

queen of the sciences and with too little training in philosophy? But with or without benefit of lecturers, there are today a great many people who have allowed themselves to be persuaded or have just absorbed the opinion – endemic in mildly intellectual circles – that there is no such thing as freedom. (If they allowed themselves to be persuaded, then obviously they *were* free to accept that opinion or reject it!) Almost everybody has some acquaintance – at second hand – with Freud's determinism, and maintains that this is what 'psychology teaches'. (It is, or surely ought to be, clear that psychology, in so far as it claims to be an exact science, cannot, in its very nature, establish freedom. It investigates mind as an external object in the same way as physical events, and therefore always in terms of causation; whereas, as we shall be seeing in a moment, causes are the opposites of actions.) Again, the popular mind is fully aware, through the Sunday papers and the media, that human behaviour is socially conditioned and in some degree related to social structures. It concludes that thought and conduct are determined by causes external to themselves.

Now admittedly there is an element of truth in this. The findings of dynamic psychology, uncovering the – at times – compulsive force of unconscious or sub-conscious motivation, the Marxist thesis that economic factors are the matrices of motives and ideologies, and – more lately – the emphasis by sociology on the omnipresence of group and cultural pressures – all these do seem to require some revision of ideas about freedom hitherto taken for granted. There can be no freedom of pure indeterminacy. We are not like the donkey between two bundles of hay. Which way we choose is not simply a toss-up. How we choose depends on the men we are – freedom must mean self-determination. And no man is an island; we do not exist in a vacuum. There are supra-personal structures of good and supra-personal structures of evil. No man is *solely* guilty for his own sins nor *solely* praiseworthy for his achievements. We are all bound up in a bundle of life together. It has to be recognized now that our freedom is more restricted in range than we had known – or than the biblical writers understood.

We do not write our choices on a clean slate and never have an unlimited field open to us – it may be no more than the choice between two evils. (It would seem that the biblical doctrine of sin now calls for some measure of reinterpretation.) But within however narrow an area – and this is what matters and what I want to emphasize – it is we who choose, and nothing else does it for us.

The key concept here is responsibility. A man may do something evil under duress – because somebody else is holding a gun at his ribs – or in ignorance of the facts of the situation and therefore not fully aware what he was doing, or through some pathological compulsion; and if so, he is not regarded as morally culpable. It was not truly 'his' act at all. This is now recognized by the courts, under the rule of diminished responsibility. (But we must not try to shelter our consciences behind the plea of 'irresistible impulse'. The allegedly irresistible impulse is the impulse that has not been resisted.) However, in most cases a man knows only too well that he need not have done what he did. *Mea culpa*, he says, *mea maxima culpa* – that is, he acknowledges responsibility. And responsibility presupposes freedom – it is, indeed, the interior moral experience which is the decisive argument for freedom. The moral command is addressed to free men. 'Thou shalt' carries with it 'Thou canst'. It is in acceptance of responsibility, in claiming to be adult, come of age, and to make his own responsible decisions, that man realizes his freedom. But responsibility means responsibility: answerability to the moral law. True freedom consists not in 'permissiveness', pretending to be our own moral arbiters – in its nature, morality cannot be permissive – but in recognizing that we are bound by a law which we may disobey but cannot alter. Kant was led to 'postulate' freedom as essentially implied in the moral will. But freedom is not merely a postulate which we have to posit in order to do ethics; it is something that we experience as reality, of which we are existentially aware in the self's own internal knowledge. And as Paul Roubiczek has argued,[3] that internal or essential knowledge is no less an apprehension of reality than the external, scientific knowledge by which we come to terms with the world outside us. Indeed the

71

strength, or what seems to be the strength, of the case against any genuine freedom of action is owing not least to confusion at this point.

The debate about freewill and determinism is as old as thought and always inconclusive. According to Milton, the archangels indulged in it, 'and found no end in wandering mazes lost'.[4] Determinism, it has been said, is a faith, and as such incapable of demonstration. It is a kind of ideal of unified knowledge, an attempt to embrace everything in a single system, known by one paradigmatic form of knowledge – that by which we know external reality. But it is surely clear that no assertion of total determinism can be true. For if all our thought is determined, so is our thought about determination. It can claim for itself no privileged exemption. Like my belief in freedom, it just happens.[5] If all-out behaviourism were the whole truth, how could anyone freely opt for behaviourism – to say nothing of claiming that theory as true?

But the whole discussion has got on to wrong lines through being bedevilled by what Gilbert Ryle, in his well-known book, has called 'the bogey of mechanism'.[6] The spectacular success of the natural sciences, working with the scientific categories of universal causation and general laws, tested by repeatable experiments, leads people to think, or to hope, that this way of knowing will be found to apply to the whole field of reality. Indeed, in order to understand any event, the mind seems compelled to assume that it occurs within the causal nexus and therefore belongs to the order of necessity, and that when we have sufficient or complete knowledge we shall see how it takes its place in the total system. If we are to be scientifically consistent, we must assume that about mental events, too. The faith of determinism, therefore, is that, however much it runs counter to common-sense or to what we think we know in our own experience, everything in the world, including the human will, must be explicable by physical causation.

Nature is a causally interlocking system which can be, ideally, read off in equations. (The indeterminancy principle in physics ought not to be quoted as any breach in this front, as though it were somehow letting freedom into nature and lending support to a 'Christian' doctrine of man. A narrow and mathematically defined unpredictablity in what is assumed to be a nexus of causal necessity is not in any way the same thing as the freedom claimed for the human will.) If we ask, What caused the man to act as he did?, we are bound to ask, What caused that cause?, and so fall into the trap of determinism. But 'the discoveries of physical science no more rule out life, sentience, purpose or intelligence from presence in the world than the rules of grammar exclude logic or style in prose'.[7] The truth is that there are realities to which causal explanations do not apply. 'Physicists may one day have found answers to all physical questions. But not all questions are physical questions.'[8] 'Why?' questions are not answerable in these terms. What we ought to ask about any intentional action is not, What caused it?, but, Why did he do it? And 'Why?' there means What was he aiming at?

Since we are both organic and spirits, we have to live in two worlds at once – the world of necessity and the world of freedom. The line between physical and metaphysical seems to run through the centre of our own being. We do not understand the relation between our minds and the infinitely complex and well-nigh incredible function of the brain cells. The materialist maintains that they are the same thing – that the thought of Plato, Shakespeare or Jesus is no more than a by-product or epiphenomenon of causally connected physical processes; and that is the too-easy short-cut of determinism. (Here is 'nothing but' revisiting us in another guise.) No account of the psychophysical inter-relation can be valid if it simply ignores the 'psycho'. Neurophysiology can describe exactly the nervous and muscular processes involved in lifting my arm and putting my hand in the till. These are what 'caused' my hand to be there. But that does not answer the question, Why is it there? An action does not just happen, it is intended. ('The question is not "What caused it?", but "Why did he do it?" ') Why my hand was in the till was because I put it there, and because I wanted to pinch the petty cash. I need not have done that, it could have been otherwise. The decision took effect through physical causes, but was not in itself causally determined.

The confusion of thought implied in all-out determinism was engagingly shown up by Gilbert Ryle in his illustration of watching a game of chess. A spectator seeing the game for the first time and trying to understand what is happening will observe that the pieces are always moved in a uniform and rigidly controlled way. A bishop cannot move from a black to a white square, but only diagonally, on the same colour. A castle can only move on a straight line, a pawn only one square at a time, and so on. It may seem to him, therefore, that every move has been predetermined in advance, laid down and prescribed before the match starts. The whole thing, he concludes, is in fact an elaborate sham. The players may think they are exercising their skill and that winning or losing depends on their thoughts, but they *can* only move their pieces in certain ways which are fixed by 'unalterable laws' and there is no scope for free play at all.

That is how it might look to the inexperienced spectator. But the players know perfectly well that he is mistaken. The rules do not decide how they move their pieces nor account for their moving them the way they do – which is, because they are aiming at winning the game. The rules are simply the agreed conditions which makes it possible for them to play chess and freely carry out their intentions. Any other game, from rugger to spillikins, would serve to illustrate the same point. What the rules of a game really constitute is a 'given' world, artificially constructed for the purpose of enjoying that game. Only within those rules can we carry out a deliberately willed and intentional exercise. (You cannot play tennis with the rules of hockey.) They are not what cause the game to be played. They do not determine how the players will play it nor how much skill or sportsmanship they will bring to it. Yet without the rules they could not be playing at all, simply because there would be no game to play.[9] But the rules do not exclude intenality, they are designed to be instrumental to it.

Similarly, the determinisms of nature can be seen to be not in opposition to freedom of human action, but its conditions. They are what makes it possible to act. Without them there could be no rational planning. Apart from the regularities of nature – if we were not sure that the sun will rise tomorrow or that like effects will always follow like causes – we could not think out or execute any purpose. Without the mechanisms of our bodies no thought could be made flesh in deed, nor any ideal aim ever be realized. Kant found that it is in obedience to the unconditional demands of the moral law that we realize our freedom as men, as rational and moral beings, against the determinisms of nature, and enter into the kingdom of ends; and that is not so far from the Christian language about finding our perfect freedom in God's service. But we do not thereby 'escape' from the order of nature in which the transcendent, absolute God is immanent. In a deeper sense, perhaps, than St Paul intended, God sent forth his Son 'born under the law.'

What is morality?

People differ about what is good: does it follow that all are equally right? Is morality merely 'subjective' – that is, in the end merely a matter of taste, so that when we say, 'Cruelty is wicked', we are really saying no more than 'I don't like it'? Or are there in truth moral standards which exist, in some sense, independently of ourselves, which we may defy but cannot alter? Here we come near the heart of the current debate about the 'objectivity' of ethics. The revolt against an authoritarian ethic is in effect a repudiation of the whole traditional notion of moral law, as though that were just arbitrarily imposed, in favour of a more liberal permissiveness in which every man is his own moral authority. (In fact, of course, it is this which is arbitrary; for if there is no recognized court of appeal, then one man's judgment is as good as another's, and anyone who says, 'This is right', is imposing his own judgment on someone else.) The Bible presupposes a moral universe, ordered and sustained by a righteous God, in which certain standards and principles are, as it were, built into the constitution, which men and societies must obey, or perish. The secular form of the biblical axiom (due in fact very largely to the Stoics) is belief in a fundamental moral law, called in religious language the law of God, written into the nature of things itself. This has been at the basis of Western civilization. It is this belief which is now being challenged by relativistic theories of morality.

The real question is, 'What is morality and to what do moral statements refer?' And that, in the end, involves ultimate questions about good and evil in the universe. But moral philosophy in its present mood is not concerned with ultimate questions of this kind. It does not presume to ask, 'What is good?' or to offer guidance about the way to live – which is, it thinks, the job of the priest or moralist rather than that of the philosopher; it confines itself to analysing the logic and to discussing the meaning of ethical propositions. What is the logical status of ethical language? That may sound remote and academic enough; but it opens up to the question we want to ask here.

When we say things like, 'This is good', what is it that we are really saying? Are such statements merely emotive? Good is a 'pro-word', it implies approval. Do we mean no more than 'I approve this'? For if so, it is simply a biographical statement: 'This arouses certain emotions in me', and in that case, there is nothing more to be said. There can be no place for any real moral argument. But people do argue about what is good, assuming that there is something there to be argued about. If A likes coffee and B likes tea, these are statements of personal preferences, and both statements are true. There is no incompatibility. But if A says 'This is good', and B says it is bad, is it possible that they can both be right? Is there not here a question of truth or falsity? Are they not referring to something 'objective' which they claim, truly or falsely, to have recognized? And if one is right, then the other must be wrong. Oddly enough, the fact that we do differ in our moral judgments, or may be mistaken in them, is one of the arguments for their 'objectivity'; they may be regarded as forms of cognition – statements about something that is real. As Miss Iris Murdoch has put it, good is part of the world, not a movable label, which can be attached to our subjective preferences.[10] That is just what relativism denies.

Not all goodness, of course, is moral goodness, though that is our immediate concern here. We can predicate goodness of all manner of things – a good pudding, a good shot in tennis, a good teacher, a good action, a good man, right up to the goodness of God. (Surely it is grotesque to suggest, as some living moral philosophers do – that 'God is good' means 'I approve of God'.) Only the two latter are strictly ethical. If we say that someone is a good cricketer, what we mean is that he plays cricket well, that he has the skills required for the game. So we could say that Edward the Confessor was a bad king (he did not do his job well), but that he was a very good man and indeed a saint. In the good man or in the morally good action the goodness is intrinsic, inherent in the person or action to which it is attributed, as it were, a moral or spiritual property. But what is it? What makes goodness good? What does the word good in itself mean? The only answer to that is, it means good. We cannot define it in terms of anything else. We cannot say, for example, that what it means is what is pleasant or what we desire or the greatest happiness of the greatest number. Stolen waters are sweet – many bad things may be pleasant; we may desire things that are evil; the greatest number in any given group might be sadists – would that make torture good? The concept of good is ultimate, irreducible and cannot be analysed into component elements. We cannot derive moral terms from non-moral; and moral experience, like religious experience, is concerned with ultimates, which can never be 'proved'. (This also applies to the moral term 'ought'. It is futile to ask, Why ought I to do my duty? My duty is what I ought to do.)

Thus when we say that something is good, we are, in part, making a factual statement (it is either good or it isn't, we may be wrong), and the same thing, of course, applies to aesthetic statements. If we say 'That picture is beautiful', we are making a judgment about the picture itself, not merely saying 'I like what I like'. But here, too, in mature life we may come to reject the aesthetic judgments of adolescence. In neither case is 'conscience' infallible.

But we certainly are not making a factual statement of the 'scientific' type like, 'This is yellow'. Ethical words are not simply descriptive, they are valuations: that is, they express the value that we find and *commend* in certain kinds of conduct.

> To evaluate 'is not to assert the existence of new special qualities'. ... Value-terms have the special function of commending, which if not done by value-terms cannot be done by any other. (Therefore) ... 'ethical judgments cannot be reduced without residuum to judgments that fall within a natural science', (and they) cannot be deduced formally from such judgments either.[11]

The logical way of stating that is that no 'is' can lead to an 'ought'. No indicative statement can yield an imperative. 'Ought' is a final and irreducible term.

Values are judgments, not simply statements of fact. 'This is yellow', and. 'This is good, or beautiful', have the same grammatical form, but their logic is altogether different. The latter commends, and affirms, that what it refers to has a *claim*, and implies that something is to be done about it. The best account of value I know is this.

> A value expresses the significance – great or small – which man ascribes to matters related to a particular activity or experience or to his life in general and thus provides him with guidance for his behaviour. Values do not exist as objects in time and space but are established by judgments – by judging things, qualities, events or actions from a personal point of view. They therefore contain both subjective and objective elements ... On the one hand, evaluation belongs to the subjective method. Values require our personal participation to come into being – that is, to become more than abstract concepts. Something must be valuable to us (or its opposite), otherwise we get to know facts and not values. A thing is not useful of itself, but for the purpose for which we need it; saving a life or taking a life are simply events unless we recognize the one deed as good and the other as evil. Similarly if there is to be any justification for calling such an everyday event as a sunset beautiful, it must be seen as such. Therefore values are not expressed by factual statements but by judgments; our personal participation and the conclusions derived from it are of the essence. On the other hand ... values ... derive from something that is objective. The fact that our judgments can be mistaken makes this clear; something may be quite useless even though we think it is useful; it is the saving of a life which is good and not our judgment of the act which makes it so;

and beauty does not lie entirely in the eye of the beholder, but resides in the object as well. Our value-judgments about things, about human behaviour and even about works of art, can be right or wrong, which shows that values possess a foundation which is independent of us.[12]

What this comes to is that value judgments, while never merely factual or empirical, are nevertheless never merely emotive, referring solely to our own attitudes, but must be accepted as genuinely cognitive, referring to something real 'outside' ourselves. And this is obviously fundamental to the 'objectivity' of morals. But ethical judgments are more than that, they require action and purport to be action-guiding. In recognizing an action as good, we thereby acknowledge that it has a claim upon us, we commit ourselves to behaving that way, we prescribe that way of behaving for ourselves, accepting it as a command or moral imperative. All imperatives are prescriptive, laying down something that is to be done, but they are not all strictly moral. 'Stop that noise' is imperative all right – and if the headmaster says it, very much so; traffic regulations (No Parking, Reduce Speed Now) tell us what to do or not to do for the sake of the public safety or convenience; but they are administrative rules rather than strictly moral *obligations*. They do not bind us in the court of conscience; they do not prescribe any kind of action unconditionally and for its own sake.

Ethical judgments command the doing of certain kinds of act, first by prescribing them for ourselves – declaring our own allegiance to them – and what we prescribe for ourselves, we prescribe for others in the same or closely similar situation. Thus moral judgments proper are universalized ('Feed the hungry', not merely 'Shut the door'), and can thus be taken as normative or action-guiding. For it is out of these various prescriptions that there is built up the body of general principles, the standards, the moral norms and maxims, which provide a group or society with directives and guidance for conduct, which each generation passes on to the next.[13]

But just how much can we mean by universal? 'So act,' said Kant, in his statement of the moral law, 'as that thou canst will thy action to be law universal.' How can we check whether what I (or any other individual or group) prescribe for myself and others is truly moral? For the various prescriptions may differ. Are there, as it were, any public reasons to which our own judgments can be submitted? Is there any universal moral *law*, which is eternal and unconditional?

Absolutes and relatives

We commonly speak about civilized ethics, the ethics of the jungle and so forth. In itself the word ethics means customs (Greek *ĕthos: ēthos* means character.) The Latin for that is *mores*, morality – that is, the behaviour of human groups. All human societies are controlled by *mores*, traditional or 'conventional' morality, enforced by the elders or other tribal authorities and regarded as being part of the nature of things; and these are closely related to social roles – we still talk about an 'unnatural' parent. Social behaviour, empirically observed, conforms to a pattern of rigid regularity – and that, not only in what people do but in their attitude to behaviour, to what is 'done' or regarded as incumbent on them. It appears that all human societies have been, at least in part, rule-directed. At this stage of human development *mores* are pre-reflective, almost instinctive; they are just what everyone does and takes for granted. It is only later – perhaps through the shock of discovering that other tribes or societies have other *mores* – that anyone starts to question them or to ask Why? It is then that morality proper begins.

But like religion, morality has a history. *Mores* and socially approved behaviour differ between one group and another and between one generation and another. Are they all equally 'true' and valid in their own historical and cultural context? Or, if not, where is the standard or criterion by which they can be tested or assessed? Are there any 'absolute' moral standards, is there any such thing as morality as such?

The study of ethics may confine itself to investigating, recording and classifying the various forms of social behaviour and the ideas associated with them, and perhaps to attempting a correlation between the *mores* of any given society and their physical health or economic efficiency or their general *ēthos* and cultural development. If it does, its function is purely descriptive; it is simply a branch of social science, concerned with facts, not with valuations. If it tries to pronounce judgment on these behaviour patterns, to affirm that one is better than another, or that all are equally good or equally bad, then it has outstripped its function as science and trespassed on the domain of moral philosophy. If the sociologist, for example proceeds from his sociological reporting to recommend some particular forms of conduct (free love or the abolition of the family) or to organize a lobby in support of it, he has forfeited his right to speak as a scientist and become what he would hate most of all to be called – an *a priori* moralist. No less so, if, as a social scientist, he preaches the doctrine of moral relativity.

Does this mean that there *are* no moral standards and that therefore there is no properly normative morality? (We have seen already that thoroughgoing relativism implies that nothing is ever really true, including, of course, the doctrine of relativism.) Or does it merely mean that the moral standards prevailing in any given society are related to its geography and history, to varying cultural and religious factors and not least – as Marx insisted – to its economy? For the latter is simply a fact of observation, too obvious to make a fuss about. (Sexual *mores* and patterns of the family have been bound up with economic changes. When women cease to be the chief producers and some form of durable wealth becomes possible, matriarchy gives way to patriarchy.) But the jump has been too quickly and lightly made from the second meaning to the former.

When civilized men first began to travel, they were fascinated by the differences – in diet, in dress, in religion, in social *mores* – between abroad and at home. (The *History* of Herodotus is packed with intriguing examples and anecdotes of this kind.) The Greek world in the fourth century BC was filled with itinerant lecturers or Sophists (from whom we obtain the objurgative word, 'sophistry') who were teaching the young men how to get on by succesful pleading or rhetoric in the courts. (Rhetoric in classical education, and particularly in late antiquity, taught how to get on without teaching how to be good – it is not an exclusively ancient phenomenon.) But as they travelled around they observed how the laws of one city differed from one another or those of any Greek city from 'the Continent'. The students would therefore have to be morally flexible, to learn how their arguments could be adjusted to different moral and legal traditions, and that would mean adopting a detached and essentially sceptical attitude towards all of them. Thus the Sophists were accused of teaching 'how to make the worse appear the better argument' – rhetorical tricks rather than stable principles; and Plato, fairly or not, accused them of undermining the bases of morality by subversive, relativistic theories. For how, they asked, are we to account for these many different standards and traditions? Is there any fundamental morality underlying them all, which exists as it were 'by nature', differently expressed in different laws and customs? What is due to nature and what to law or convention? Or was the answer a radical moral scepticism – that nothing is due to nature at all, but that all moral standards are arbitrary conventions, imposed by the haves on the have-nots, or by those in power on the lower orders? Is justice – as Plato makes one of the Sophists say 'nothing but (here again!) the interest of the stronger'? If so, of course, there are no normative standards and the young may conclude that everything is permitted.

In the simpler, pre-industrial society, in which there was an agreed value-system and a common moral vocabulary, and in which everyone had his appointed place and his recognized social role, it was still possible to see morality largely in terms of 'my station and duties'. Christian children were taught that their duty to God – i.e. the demand of morality itself – was 'to do my duty in that state of life into which it shall please God to call me'. But with a vastly increased population, in a far more complex and pluralist society, men have to occupy many different stations with different and often conflicting duties. Most men today have a number of different roles – in the home, in business, in local government, in their clubs and leisure-time activities. Each man in his time plays many parts – not successively but contemporaneously; and all these roles have their own requirements and their own internal standards of expectation. He may frequently find himself torn between them. The standards that he tries to teach his children seem to be incompatible with those to which he has to conform in the rat-race if he is to earn enough money to keep the family. The ethic that he must accept as a politician may be one that he would disdain in his private life. There seem to be half a score of different moralities. Are there, then, any rules other than roles? Can there be any single, uniform moral law which is applicable in a pluriform society?

The early anthropologists were impressed by the immense variety of *mores* and the wide divergence of socially approved standards as between one society and another. Their reaction to that was moral and cultural relativism – as though what is good in one social group or culture, polygamous African tribesmen, for example, might be bad in the world of monogamous Europeans. Sociologists have shown how different values tend to be characteristic of different strata in the class-structure: the professional class, for example, with the values and virtues of the grammar-school prefect, and the working-class boy from a 'school you have never heard of' – and they draw the same relativist conclusion. Moreover, as we saw in the previous paragraph, different moral standards appear to operate from one day or one hour to another within the experience of the individual – and this, too, seems to point towards relativity. But here, once again, we must notice the confusion between mere description and moral evaluation, between social science and moral philosophy. To observe that different groups of people – or the same people in their changing roles – do in fact rule their lives by different principles, is not at all incompatible with believing that there are right principles to be known. You can, logically, be a descriptive relativist and yet believe that there are absolute norms. I save quoted above Miss Murdoch's movable label'. As she herself points out, Milton's Lucifer moved the label the whole width of the universe: 'Henceforth evil, be thou my good.' And that is more than a line in *Paradise Lost*. A film was recently shown in Piccadilly, with the usual sexy girl on the poster and the title *Do not deliver us from evil*. That is not 'permissive' morality, or morality of any kind. It is Satanism. In effect, it denies the goodness of good and puts the devil in the place of God. It is what Jesus seems to have meant, in reply to a charge of performing black magic, by blasphemy against the Holy Spirit.

The best known statement of 'absolute' morality is that of Kant's Categorical Imperative. The one thing supremely and absolutely good is the good will, which acts out of respect for the moral law, with no other motive, even desiring to do it. This is valid for all men at all times and places, irrespective of circumstances – indeed, this *is* morality, this is absolute. Now this is perfectly normative in the sense of defining what conditions must be present to make any act a genuinely moral act. But it gives us hardly any information about what kinds of act are good, what ends we should aim at or how we should try to live. It has hardly any positive content; it is duty devoid of any particular duties. Kant supplies a normative morality for the individualistic society which was then beginning to emerge, by detaching the moral imperative from contingent political and social circumstances. This makes the individual morally sovereign and independent of all external authorities, in tune with the general temper of the Enlightenment (and thus provided the philosophical background for the individualism of Protestant ethics and the fatal breach between private and public morality which was so disastrous in later German history). But it is an almost entirely formal ethic. The strength of this lofty and austere philosophy is to entrench that sense of *obligation* which is integral to genuine moral experience, to insist that the moral law *is* a law, which cannot be twisted to suit our inclinations or changed to suit changes of taste or circumstance. But its weakness is that it is conceived on such a high level of abstraction as to fail to be action-guilding in the concrete. It is an ethic of motive or intention. But if we ask what acts are right, the only principle Kant can offer is that

84

they are such acts as we can will to be law universal, to apply to all men (truth-telling, promise-keeping, etc.), whatever may be their actual situation. But we are given no positive sense of direction pointing to the ends which the good life should seek, and no qualitative criterion of values. The Christian statement of absolute moral law as set forth in the two great commandments invests good acts with positive content and gives an unfailing sense of moral direction. But separate duty from any duties, and almost anything not forbidden may be seen as categorically binding. In that case, what claims to be absolute moral law appears to offer no moral guidance at all.

This is what your relativist will quote at you. It appears to him that an absolute morality must be so vacuous as be morally useless. All that makes it difficult for 'modern man' to belief in a transcendent God operates to make him suspicious of absolute values. Both seem to inhabit a kind of mental stratosphere which is impenetrable by our knowledge, so remote from our mundane experience and our down-to-earth moral decisions as to be, for all practical purposes, irrelevant. And it must be admitted, as we have just seen, that the nearer a moral principle approaches to being universal and absolute, the more formal and abstract it may appear to be; in this it resembles the laws of the natural sciences.

But modern man has been misled by a misunderstanding of language. A transcendent God does not mean one who is in himself totally unknowable or who has nothing whatever to do with the world. It means a God who is other than the world – we cannot speak about the world and man, but can speak about the world and God – who is self-subsistent and not dependent on any reality 'outside' himself. So an absolute standard does not mean one which is unrelated to any actual circumstances. What could such a standard conceivably be? A standard for nothing is not a standard. Being a standard involves being a standard for something which is the case. No standard is absolute in the sense of applying to no circumstances whatever. It is as useless as a theatre ticket which applies to no particular seat. An absolute standard means 'one by which everything else is measured, not having itself to be tested by reference to anything else',[14] or, in other words, underived and unconditional. So an absolute ethic cannot mean an ethic irrelevant to particular cases, but one that is normative for all cases and by which all actions can be valued according to their degree of approximation to it, but whose standards are intrinsic and 'autonomous', not tested by anything beyond themselves. It certainly does not mean a list of things which everybody must do or refrain from doing altogether regardless of circumstances – there can be no acts regardless of circumstances, and a laid-on morality is not morality. That is, to be sure, how it is represented by opponents and critics of the Christian ethic. But what the Christian commandments are concerned with is normative principles rather than with a rule-book. As we shall see, I hope, in a later section, the 'new moralities' rest on a mistake.

Morality and religion

What do we mean when we say we 'ought' to do something? What is the source of authority in ethics? Once we have prescribed something to ourselves, or accepted a standard as having a claim upon us, we know that we are under an obligation. The language of morals speaks in the imperative. It does not say, 'Would you feel inclined to do this?' It says 'Thou shalt', or, 'Thou shalt not', and the fundamental moral imperatives, formulated for Jews and Christians in the Decalogue, have been more or less constant throughout recorded history. (No sane man, as Lord Hailsham said in a broadcast, would suggest writing them in reverse: Thou shalt kill, steal, bear false witness, etc.) Moral standards present themselves as law, and if we violate them we feel guilty. But what is the source or ground of this obligation? What invests the moral imperative with authority ? A law seems to presuppose a lawgiver; and a civilization imbued with the Bible has had no hesitation about the answer: the commandments are the commandments of God, and the moral law issues from the will of God. Popular Christian teaching has taken for granted that morality depends on religion and that ethics, therefore, derives from theology.

But both in philosophical and religious circles this is now exposed to some rather searching criticism, and some discussion seems to be needed here. How is religion related to morality?

Philosophers urge that no indicative statement, even if it is a statement about God, can ever yield a true moral imperative: *Ought* cannot be derived from *is*. This is obviously true in logic, though it is not the last word. But the real objection is at a deeper level, and concerns what is called the autonomy of ethics. An autonomous state is one that makes its own laws, subject to no jurisdiction outside itself. And morality, it is objected, is autonomous in the sense that its authority is intrinsic to it and is subject to nothing beyond it or external to it – not even to the will of God. Things are not made good by being willed by God; they are good and right because they are good and right. Good is ultimate and irreducible – as I have myself already insisted. If we try to support the authority of morals by appeal to any 'higher' authority, we shall be debasing the moral currency and violating its own inherent autonomy. We may also be tainting the springs of moral motive by implied suggestions of future reward and punishment. 'Religious morality is infantile'[15]: 'I ought to do this because Daddy says so', and that is not strictly a moral reason at all. Ethics cannot be made to depend on theology without thereby ceasing to be ethical.

Here we have the position of secular humanism in its attack on a God-oriented morality: by 'dragging God into it' you debase morality. What is the reply from the Christian side? There is first a fairly obvious linguistic point. When we speak about God's commands, we are using the word only analogically, and we ought no doubt to be far more careful than we always are in the way we use the analogy: God is not a celestial sergeant-major. Further, what the word God means for Christians is absolute and inexhaustible goodness – Goodness itself – and therefore what he 'commands' is good and cannot be anything else but good: there is no suggestion of arbitrary *fiat*. But we have to know what we mean by good before we can say God's commands are good; and that knowledge is not derived from belief in God; it is, in a real sense, prior to that belief, and one of the major reasons for belief. We are not saying, or should not be saying, that good *means* being willed by God.

When Mrs Margaret Knight goes around crusading about morals without religion, Christians tend to get hot under the collar and pulpits are thumped with appeals to return to religion in order to save us from moral collapse. When I was younger I was myself shocked by it and preached eloquent sermons in protest. It seemed to me then to be undermining the foundations both of morality and religion. Now that I am older and have thought and read more, I realize that there is nothing to be shocked about. Neither St Paul nor Augustine would have denounced it. The mainstream Christian tradition, from St Paul to St Thomas, to Hooker and Joseph Butler, has always maintained that by the light of reason man can discern the basic moral principles, can differentiate between good and evil, apart from any specific belief in God. There are millions of good men who are not religious. Some of the no-God humanists themselves are among the most highly moral people alive. ('Good men without God' are no problem to the Christian, who believes in the incarnate Logos as the true Light that lighteth every man.) It does not need Christianity to tell us that it is better to be kind than beastly. Theism can and does qualify morality and bring into it new depths and delicacy, but it cannot create it. Morality is autonomous. We who inherit the biblical tradition can hardly conceive a non-ethical religion – against which the Old Testament is a sustained polemic. The Christian religion is ethical through and through. Worship and the good life are inseparable. But its ethical claim binds us in its own right. Religion, moreover, constantly needs purgation by a genuinely independent moral criticism. Without that, religion has too often brought flaming moral evil with it and inflicted terrible suffering, on mankind – (human sacrifice, inquisition, suppression of freedom, religious wars, etc.).

So much for the demarcation dispute as between two fields of enquiry. Ethics is not a department of theology. Its autonomy must be recognized and respected. But there is a bigger question involved in the humanist criticism of Christian morality. Humanists claim that man is the measure of all things and that there is nothing higher than man. Morality, therefore, has to be vindicated entirely within the human dimension and without any reference to a transcendent God. Any recognition of God would rob man of his human dignity – for he would not then be the highest of things – and subordinate morals to some trans-human reality and so rob the moral law of its majesty. The question is whether such an attempt is viable. Ethics may be independent of theology, but does our moral experience make sense on any purely humanistic assumptions? If we acknowledge a moral obligation independent of our desires and wills, is not that an admission that there is something higher than man to which he is answerable? Moral experience does not exist in a vacuum, but in a real world, the total human world, and (in so far as man is organic to nature) the natural world as well. How is it that moral principles are applicable – that they 'work' – in the actual empirical world? Can we divorce moral obligation from the way man himself is and the way the world is? If, as we have seen, our subjective values have nevertheless an objective grounding – for otherwise there could be no discussion of them – that would seem to imply that, at the end of the day, they are built into the structure of the cosmos and indeed (since values require mind to recognize them) that they are held in a supra-human consciousness.

If we start by assuming that there is no God, that the universe is morally blind and neutral, unconcerned with our values and our striving, unresponsive to the claim we make upon it, then our moral experience is self-contradictory and our moral selfhood absurd: it makes no sense. But if we do believe in a rational universe – and if not, we must throw out our science – it can be argued that 'ought' must, in the end, be grounded in the ultimate 'is'. That is what Christian theism affirms.

It is not only the moral law whose autonomy is alleged to be invaded by a theologically based ethic, but also man himself as a moral agent. In praising one action and blaming another, in calling one right and the other wrong, we assume that the doer himself was responsible. It was he who did it, and it was his act, issuing freely from his own choice, not determined by anything external to him. If it was not in every sense his own act, then it was not in the full sense a moral act, and no moral judgment on it will lie. But if Christians drag in the notion of God's grace assisting or enabling a good act, we cannot attribute it solely to the agent. He was being coached or helped from another source. His autonomy has thus been eroded and with it the moral quality of his action. Indeed, there is a suggestion of cheating: it is too much as though a headmaster gave tips to a favourite pupil in his O levels. But just how free, it may be asked, are we? Is the agent quite as autonomous as they make out? We know only too well that a man may be capable of knowing quite clearly what he ought to do and yet be unable to do it because of some other 'law in our members'. Here we encounter the 'bondage of the will' from which we are set free to be ourselves, which can only be by a power beyond ourselves. A deeper analysis of moral experience seems to drive us back on the need for grace – whether or not it is consciously accepted – if there are to be good men at all.

There is a further reflection of the same kind, arising out of the fact of moral conversion. Somebody who has been hitherto a 'bad' man, identifying his will with what is evil, may be converted and become a 'good' man, identifying his will with what is good. But how can this be, if he is self-sufficient and self-contained as a moral agent? Can an evil will generate a good will?[16]

The more you reflect, the more you are led to see that moral experience is not self-explanatory; and that though it is autonomous in its own right, it is always pointing beyond itself into the religious dimension. It appears to be putting to us further questions which morality by itself cannot answer. Moral failure evokes the consciousness of guilt, but morality can know nothing of forgiveness – to 'justify the sinner' in court is immoral. So too, there is the problem of freedom, which reaches into a transcendent plane. The point has been well put by Gibson Winter:

Morality always points beyond itself, although moral questions may be pursued without engaging in reflection on ultimates. Freedom, self-awareness, and self-transcendence are presupposed by morality and point beyond morality.

There is not only our own guilt, but the fact that the consequences may fall on the innocent.

Such problems form the 'religious' backdrop of the existential question in social ethics. Interpreting religion in the broadest sense as man's ultimate concern, we can affirm that morality raises questions of guilt and tragedy which it cannot contain ... Religion qualifies the moral imperative with its ultimate vision, while sustaining the relative autonomy of the moral order. Man's moral possibilities and problems are founded in his freedom. They cease to be moral if they are grounded elsewhere than in this freedom. However, freedom points man to problems of reality in which both freedom and morality are disclosed as absurd or ultimately significant. At this point of intersection, the moral question of meaning presses towards a religious answer. By the same token, man's moral awareness challenges his religious symbols and his views of divine goodness in an evil world.[17]

But I think we can fairly go further than this and affirm not only that morality points to religion, but that it discloses the object of religion. Morality is, as it has been phrased, 'that side of religion which can be discussed, and that implies that it can be discussed independently of religion'.[18] Moral experience and religious experience are different forms of spiritual awareness or – to use a topical metaphor – different 'channels' through which ultimate meanings are transmitted, but they bring us transmissions of the same reality. Each of them has its own laws and structures, and we must not pretend that they are identical, or – as is now increasingly the fashion – try to transform religion into ethics. But the two streams meet in that totally ethical theism which is presupposed in the Bible and Christianity.

All our apprehensions of value – intellectual, moral or aesthetic – lead on to further and fuller apprehensions. The more truth we discover, the more there is to be known. Recognition of beauty, whether in art or nature, can never be more than a partial intimation of a perfect beauty yet to be revealed.

Our loves, even married love at its best, are but fragmentary and imperfect realizations of a 'perfect Love, all human thought transcending'. Whatever we may achieve in our moral growth beckons us on to higher peaks beyond it, and we cannot rest in anything short of perfection. All values, in short, are disclosures of absolute value, all forms of good of Goodness-in-itself, and are thus, in their measure, disclosures of the Absolute.

The absolute is part of our experience and is revealed by experience alone; it cannot be established, confirmed or tested by anything else.[19]

It *is*. This is most clearly the case in our moral experience. Here we know that we can understand ourselves only as being under an obligation to a claim which is unconditional, un-derived and unqualified by anything else; and is not that just what we mean by the Absolute? But absolute goodness which is unconditioned, underived and self-subsistent in personal being is known to religion as God. Morality and religion are distinguishable as two authentic forms of experience; but in both we are in encounter with God.

Morality need not be derived from religion or – in principle – from anything else. But it is clear that men's moral notions and the general content of their moral judgments do derive from their cultural and social contexts and – most conspicuously – from their religion. So it makes perfectly good sense to speak about Christian ethics, or Jewish, Buddhist or Islamic ethics. What distinguishes one from the other is its theology, its distinctive beliefs about God and man's relation to him. Christian morals depend on Christian theology. You can have a high standard of morality without believing in the God of Christians and without any positive attitude to Jesus. What you cannot have is the Christian way of living.

Christian morals and 'new moralities'

Christian ethics, then, are essentially religious ethics. As the Christian religion rests on revelation, so its morality is a 're-vealed' morality – not something that we have thought up by our own philosophizing but something *given* by God through Jesus Christ, and therefore something that man cannot alter: morality absolute and final. (What Christians mean by the finality of Christ himself or of Christian ethics, is that they can never be superseded, not that there is nothing more to be learnt about them.) As such it is universal – for men as men. This is the point of humanist objection to it. To call it 'revealed' only reinforces all the current suspicion of absolutes. It suggests the will of an arbitrary despot or a code of rules handed down from above, far too inflexible and far too rigid to be relevant to changing situations or the actual conflicts and tragedies of man's life. It is thought to be something 'inhuman' and remote, and the general feeling is that Christian moralists will react to any concrete moral difficulties with stock reactions and conventional judgments lacking in real human understanding. Hence the demand for a more permissive morality, already discussed at the beginning of this chapter.

But this partly rests on misunderstanding. The Christian ethic is certainly a commandment in so far as it rests on God's will for men; and, as someone has said, if what God wills for men is not to be *obeyed*, then he is not God. But it is not a static code of conduct. No authority, human or divine, can tell us exactly what we are to do in situations that have not yet arisen. If Jesus had consented to legislate – which he steadfastly refused to do – it would have been out of date many years ago. It must be admitted that Christians have at times given the impression of caring more about the breaking of rules than about the moral quality of an action; and that may reduce a creative and dynamic ethic to respectability. But Mrs Grundy is not a Christian saint. Jesus offended the moralists of his day by his insistence on going behind the rules to the moral realities which they exist to safeguard. (But this does not mean that we can dispense with rules.)

Jesus himself was a man of his own time – a Jew in Palestine in the first century in a country under Roman occupation – a fact by which Jewish daily life was dominated. He spoke to men out of a certain situation which was culturally and historically conditioned. He was not speaking directly to us, in a world which he did not and could not have foreseen. But what he said has an eternal quality, revealing ultimate meanings in life which provide guiding principles for action which endure from one generation to another. But what are absolute are the eternal principles. What they require to be actually done may not be the same for twentieth-century Christians as for those who first heard him speak. Following Christ's example cannot mean doing exactly the same things as Jesus did; it means being faithful to his spirit as disclosed in his recorded actions, and his vision of what life really is.

In the popular mind Christian morality means carrying out the teaching of Jesus and particularly the Sermon on the Mount. People talk of 'applying' the Sermon on the Mount, almost equated with the Golden Rule – one wonders at times whether they have ever read it – as though it were a pot of paint or wallpaper which could be 'applied' to any and every surface. If it were taken as law for a modern state, it would bring civilization to an end. Yet that does not mean that the Christian ethic is a wonderful but impracticable ideal which will not work in business or politics. Talk about Christian ideals is futile and reduces Christianity, in effect, to an utterly ineffective 'if only people were nicer than they are the world would be nicer than it is.' 'If only everybody became Christian ethic is a wonderful but impracticable ideal which true: the technical problems would still remain to be solved and religion alone cannot tell us how to solve them). But the Sermon is not to be taken as legislation (even though St Matthew may have so understood it). It describes the spirit in which men must live – a quality and direction, as Dodd puts it – if they are to enter into the kingdom of God. It is a code not of rules, but of dispositions.

About all this more must be said later. But if we want to know what Jesus has bequeathed to us and what is really implied in the Christian ethic, we must look first not at his teaching preserved in the gospels – and already edited – but at the earlier writings, the epistles. These are key-documents, for they provide us, casually, as it were, and unintentionally – they were never intended to be Holy Scripture – with the most

94

reliable picture we have of original Christianity in action.[20]

The Christian church did not create morality, as some Christians so oddly appear to think. The moral experience of mankind is cumulative, and you cannot create an ethic 'out of nothing'. No teacher is writing on a blank sheet. Jesus himself, as we shall see in a moment, was not propounding a new system of ethics; he was working on and within what was there already. The church had behind it the legacy of Judaism, the great tradition of Greek moral philosophy, the popular ethical teaching of the Stoics and the whole gathered store of moral wisdom commonly handed down in age-old proverbs. The church took over the best it could find in all these – quite a lot in the ethical sections of the epistles would have been accepted by non-believers. But into these great moral commonplaces the church introduced a new depth and richness, new scales of values and qualitative standards, a new valuation of human life itself, in the light of the new thing which it proclaimed, which was to transform morality from within, so that the old commandment became a new commandent. What 'Moses' – or Plato – had taught was not abrogated, but it was redeemed and refined. The new thing which it proclaimed was the fact of Christ – his life and teaching, his death and resurrection – which had changed the whole human situation and brought men into new relationship with God.

That was seen to entail that men had now been brought into new relationship with one another within the koinōnia of the Spirit. A new way of life had been disclosed in Jesus and new possibilities of living opened for them if they were 'raised with Christ into newness of life'. (Christian ethics are resurrection ethics.) The gospel is a gospel about God and the glad tidings of reconciliation, and that is what the New Testament proclaims. It is not a manual of Christian ethics ('If Christianity,' said Blake, 'were ethics, then Socrates is the saviour'), but a setting forth of God's work in man through Christ. Out of that flows an interior transformation, a radical transvaluation of values, a changed attitude to life as a whole, to God, the world, the self and other people, a deepening and refinement of character and that distinctive quality of spirit for which the New Testament shorthand is *agape*. And the gospel is always verified in action and in the way men treat one another. The general layout of the epistles, that is, the missionary letters or 'pastorals' from the father-founders to the tiny churches established in the Mediterranean area, begins by presenting the gospel message itself, and then proceeds to give practical direction about the way Christians ought to live and how various groups within the church – husbands and wives, parents and children, masters and slaves – must learn to treat one another.

Here we get a glimpse – never meant for our eyes – of the first churches, nearest to the source, learning how to work out a Christian life-pattern. It was not an immediate or automatic process. There were many failures and even moral scandals, and not all reached the true Christian level. (Were all the first Christians monogamists? I wonder.) They were not responsible for 'those without', but within the *koinonia* of redemption they were responsible for one another. The *koinonia*, therefore, had to be governed by rules. With all his polemic against the law, St Paul issues imperative commands: I command you in the name of the Lord Jesus. Bear one another's burdens and so fulfil the law of Christ; and so on. The appeal is to an absolute moral standard, a Christian law, God-given and authoritative.

Now behind all that St Paul and the other writers have to say to their converts, there stands a Person, and his lineaments recognizably show through. There are some, but only a few direct quotations from his words to support their directions. But it is much more what they take for granted – the qualities of mind and spirit which they admire and hold up for emulation, the ideal of human perfection which they assume, their understanding of what goodness really is. All the time they are talking about a Person and the new thing which he has brought into human life: 'Forgiving one another as Christ forgave you'; 'Let this mind be in you which was also in Christ Jesus; though he was rich, yet for our sake he became poor'. What the ethic presented in the epistles comes to is growing into those qualities of character and those responses to God and man which are open to those who are reborn 'in Christ' (cf. Gal. 4.1, 'Till Christ be formed in you'). It is the Christian life in action and is therefore, in one sense, always in the making.

This is how, I suggest, the New Testament presents it. Here is a standard of absolute perfection – and nothing lower than that can be God's will for us – yet all is dynamic, creative and redemptive. This is miles away from the codified moralism which we find a generation later in the *Didache* and the sub-apostolic writings. And no doubt the church has always been in danger of missing the many-splendoured thing by trying to formalize and codify it as though the fountain of life were a legal instrument – and making the Christian ethic a list of rules. When that happens, obeying the law of Christ tends to mean the minimum we can get away with. The challenging note at the heart of it has gone dead.

These letters were written for those who first read them, not as Holy Scripture for posterity. They are therefore historically conditioned. It is vain to seek in them a blueprint for twentieth-century Christian behaviour. And this is true also about Jesus' own teaching. When we read it in the context of today, we are almost shocked by its drastic limitations. There is nothing here about economics, about science or industry or capitalism, the bomb or the pill or women's lib, or any of the problems which we have to meet. How then, people ask, can he be claimed as the final and absolute moral authority if he seems to have so little to say about many of our most urgent moral questions? But this is part and parcel of the concentration, the so-called 'scandal of particularity', implied in a historical incarnation. God is revealed not in mankind in general but in this one particular man – the infinite in the finite and fragmentary, absolute goodness in one conditioned life.

So in his teaching he has not told us everything. What he told us was the one thing needful. What he gave us was the one pearl of great price which determines the value of all other pearls – the disclosure of what life really is in its essential quality and meaning – in scriptural language, eternal life –

when it is in right relationship with God. That is the heart and core of the Christian ethic, and it is the burden of everything he said.

He came proclaiming the good news of the kingdom, and the laws of the kingdom are the laws of God's being. The right way of living is 'the reality principle', that which corresponds with reality, with the structure of life as God designs it, the way of obedience to the will of God. As a Jew, Jesus accepted the Jewish law. He did not claim to have superseded the Decalogue. He did not invent the two great commandments; he said that they were what fundamentally mattered in the complex corpus of the Torah, and the criterion of all morality; 'There is no other commandment greater than these.' For in all his teaching he was pressing back behind the formal external command to its inner meaning, to what it really implied – something far more profound and more demanding than rabbinical Judaism had understood. This was not the teaching of a new ethic. It was a critique of the traditional ethic, which he sought to deepen and purify. He did not provide a new set of rules or tell people exactly what to do. 'Go and do thou likewise' – but do what? What he taught was the eternal principles in the light of which men must make their own decisions in freedom and responsibility before God. It is utterly impossible to confine the creative spirit of Jesus in a code. His has been called a morality without rules. It is a radically religious ethic, 'Be merciful because God is merciful'; and it is also radically perfectionist, 'Be perfect even as your Father in heaven is perfect'. So it is, in effect, a critique of all ethics by a standard of absolute perfection. 'When you have done all that is commanded you, say, we are unprofitable servants.' Whatever standards or moral insights we may have attained, there is still more to be realized. The Christian ethic is not a completed system. While it is absolute in its obligation, its content will be continually revised, deepened, purified and enriched through the presence of Christ and the guidance of the Spirit.

But if all this is true, how can it be normative or action-guiding for twentieth-century men? And further, how far can we be justified in talking about the Christian moral *law*? Is not spontaneity of the very essence of the teaching of Jesus and of the Christian life?

What we commonly call the new morality, both in its Christian and non-Christian forms, is a revolt against formal codification as incompatible with true moral freedom and with every man's rightful demand to be himself and 'not to be governed by other peoples rules, even though they call them God's law'.[21]

What existentialists call authentic living is to be authentically oneself, the self that one is and nobody else is, realizing one's own unique potentialities of existence. Ethically, this must imply a complete openness to the future. To conform to the past, to be guided by norms concerning what one 'ought' to do, is bad faith and denial of one's own authenticity. The future calls us to create in the light of the emerging situation what at present is not there at all. Thus there can be no moral rules. To be man is freedom, and freedom (says Sartre) is 'nothing' – a gap to be filled, a potentiality to be realized as situations disclose their emergent claims. There are thus no eternal or normative values; we have to create our values as we go along, out of our own inner existential freedom.

The first and obvious criticism of this will stress its unmitigated individualism. We are only personal beings at all in society, that is, in inter-personal relationships, and authentic living cannot be isolated from a right relation to the common life. Moreover, if the will can have no content, if we can never know what we are aiming at, we seem to be not far from moral nihilism, overwhelmed and drowned in the Nothing. One is not surprised that Sartre, in his later period, has identified himself with the Communist programme; for this, though it meant throwing over his earlier principles, has given him some positive end to live for.

The tension between traditional Christian ethics and the various versions of new morality turns on the assumption that absolute norms or principles must involve rigid and unchanging rules. The latter, we saw, are incompatible with the spirit and ethos of Jesus' own teaching. The love-commandment implies spontaneity. Yet how can an ethic that claims to be universal provide norms for action in society if it cannot be set forth in the form of general laws? Situation ethics is a breakaway from abstract laws and generalizations to concrete ethical decisions. Acts are not right acts *in vacuo*; an act is right in a given situation. What we have to do is to ascertain what the situation is and requires, and what it requires is the morally right act. This implies that a morally right action is essentially spontaneous rather than rule-guided. This has a Christian sound about it and some Christian writers, like Joseph Fletcher (and Bishop Robinson), have developed a Christian situational ethic. This, they maintain, is a recovery of the ethic taught and exemplified by Jesus from the legalism and formality with which traditional teaching has overlaid it. (But legalism does not mean obeying the law; it means making the law an end in itself. The younger liberal Protestant writers have got legalism on the brain.) Love, they say, is essentially spontaneous. The Christian procedure is therefore first of all to find out what the situation is, and then just to do 'the most loving thing'. But what kinds of things does love require? How do we know, in a given situation, what the most loving thing really is? Can we get on without some guiding rules?

It astonishes me that Christian writers suppose that we can act from Christian love and that human love has ultimate, absolute value. It astonishes me that Professor Braithwaite can announce, as a 'declaration of policy', his decision to 'act in an agapeistic way', reinforced by the stories about Jesus.[22]

Are we men capable of pure love? Do we think we can love as Jesus loved? Love is a gift and we too often spoil it by our own waywardness and selfishness. Jesus said that his new commandment was 'to love one another as I have loved you'. Christian *agape* is a response to a love given to us by God in Christ. 'We love because he first loved us.' It is not a 'natural' human disposition. And because what love implies may too often cut across our natural inclinations, it presents itself as commandment, as law.

But further than this, what *is* the situation? It often appears to be superficially analysed.

The real situation is likely to be seen as involving more than the emotions of the principal actors in the immediate drama. The interests of society and of future generations will almost always deserve serious consideration and the wisdom of society and of past generations will almost always deserve more attention that the individual in his enthusiasm is liable to offer at once.[23]

How can situation ethics help us in the complicated decisions involved in nuclear weapons, in ecological conservation, in the problem of biological engineering, in the structures of multi-racial societies, or of contraceptives, abortion or euthanasia? Here, for example, is a girl in distress because of an unwanted pregnancy. The obviously loving thing to do – in her current jargon, the compassionate thing – is to relieve her of her distress by terminating it without questions asked. But what is the loving thing for the other person immediately involved, the unborn baby? And if you give licence for abortion on any other than therapeutic grounds are you not, in effect, giving licence for infanticide and endangering that respect for the sanctity of human life on which you base your maxim of people first? The clamour for abortion on demand is leaving out all those wider considerations.[24] There are two great commandments, not only one. We are trying to work with the second alone, and the first is thought to be no longer necessary.[25] But it means that in loving the neighbour we have to consider not only the loving thing in this particular case but its effect in all cases in the community and in God's world as a whole – or, in other words, to universalize. Thus there cannot be love without laws.

I end by quoting one of the leading authorities in the field of Christian ethics, Paul Ramsey:

How can Christians nourish the seeds of a wider social responsibility while seeming to praise only acts and never rules that embody personal responsibility between the two parties to sexual relations? Plainly, the waywardness of the human heart works against any *ethos*, customs, or laws that are generally good for all, and not merely against the 'traditional code'. Protestant Christian ethics is often too profoundly personal to be socially relevant if in this is included even a minimum of concern for the social habits and customs of a people. Ordinarily, we do not take Christian ethics with enough seriousness to illumine the path men, women, and *society* should follow today. This suggests that only some form of rule-agapism, and not only act-agapism, can be consistent with the elaboration of a Christian's social responsibilities. No social morality ever was founded, or ever will be founded, upon a situational ethic.'[26]

The various versions of situation ethics are in effect moralities of intention. So was that of Abelard and Héloïse. The intention is all, it is the motive from which the act derives its moral quality. If you are sincere, say the young people, isn't that all that matters? If the boy loves the girl, isn't it all right? But this is just a mistake in moral philosophy. Many evil deeds have been terribly 'sincere'. Motives affect our judgment on the agent – in so far, that is, as we can ever know them – but motives do not make actions good or bad. No purely intentional morality, whether in Kant or the latest progressive paperback, can provide the base for a Christian social ethic.[27]

NOTES

1. It is often objected that the early church accepted the institution of slavery. As an insignificant, outlawed minority in a vast empire it clearly could not do anything else and it was not conscious of any responsibility for the regeneration of secular society. Its responsibility was for its own members, many of whom were slaves in the world, but within the church brethren in Christ. Within the church slaves could be bishops. It is clear that some Christians owned slaves. Did they set them free? We do not know (but here Philemon is a key document). Christian funds were used to buy the emancipation of slaves, as for the redemption of prisoners. What Christianity did in the early days was to inculcate a new attitude to slaves, which was in the end to prove incompatible with the institution of slavery. What is appalling is that it took so long, that the church continued for so many centuries to condone the abomin-

ations of the trade and merely sent missionaries to the plantations. Unfortunately the church cannot claim to have been in the lead of abolition. The French revolution got in first. But the ignominious record of the churches does not alter what is really inherent in the Christian doctrine of man.

2. Wolfhart Pannenberg, *The Apostles' Creed*, p. 117.

3. Paul Roubiczek, *Ethical Values in the Age of Science*, Cambridge University Press, 1969, chs. IV and V.

4. Milton, *Paradise Lost*, II, 555.

5. See above on relativism, p. 34.

6. Gilbert Ryle, *The Concept of Mind*, Hutchinson, 1967, p. 79.

7. Ryle, op. cit., p. 19.

8. Ryle, ibid., p. 76.

9. Ibid., pp. 77–9.

10. Iris Murdoch, *The Sovereignty of Good*, Routledge and Kegan Paul, 1970, p. 3.

11. Ian T. Ramsey, 'Moral Judgments and God's Commands', in *Christian Ethics and Contemporary Philosophy*, SCM Press, 1966, pp. 165, 156, quoting A. C. Ewing.

12. Roubiczek, op. cit., pp. 219f.

13. This is in effect the position of R. M. Hare in his well known book *The Language of Morals*, Oxford University Press, 1952.

14. G. F. Woods, *A Defence of Theological Ethics*, Cambridge University Press, 1966, p. 38.

15. P. Nowell Smith, *Ethics*, Blackwell, 1957.

16. These last two paragraphs depend on G. F. Woods, op. cit., pp. 15f.

17. Gibson Winter, *Social Ethics*, SCM Press, 1968, pp. 8ff.

18. Roubiczek, op. cit., p. 28.

19. Ibid., p. 72.

20. For fuller discussion of this see my *Christian Ethics and Secular Society*, Hodder and Stoughton, 1966, pp. 70ff., and the references.

21. On this see, among many other books, a brilliant study by G. R. Dunstan, *Not Yet the Epitaph*, Exeter University Press, 1968.

22. Braithwaite is only to be understood against the background of Matthew Arnold: religion is 'morality tinged with emotion'.

23. David Edwards, *Religion and Change*, Hodder and Stoughton, 1969, p. 341. He observes that 'people before principles is still a principle'.

24. A very able article by Ronald Butt in *The Times*, 1 February 1973, about euthanasia, draws attention to the warning conveyed by

the way, unintended by Parliament, in which the abortion act is working out in practice.

25. See on this, John Selwyn Gummer, *The Permissive Society: Fact or Fantasy?*, Cassell, 1971, p. 151.

26. Paul Ramsey, *Deeds and Rules in Christian Ethics*, Scribner, New York, ²1967, p. 20.

27. For further reading, in addition to the books already mentioned, the best single book for background reading in the whole subject now available is probably G. F. Thomas, *Christian Ethics and Moral Philosophy*, Scribner, New York, 1972.

5 | Other-worldliness and secularity

Worldliness and godliness

'Other-worldly' is one of the dirty words now. Christianity has too long been dominated by what has been dubbed extricationist theology, overmuch concerned with getting people out of this wicked world into another – a better land, far, far away – or with 'going to heaven when we die'. So were the ancient mystery religions, which offered a post-mortem salvation and to that extent could be branded as escapist. It is possible to concentrate so exclusively on what happens to the soul after death as to seem to drain this present life of meaning and to weaken our sense of social responsibility. It is too suggestive of pie in the sky. Against all that we are now in full reaction. Involvement is the blessed word today. The Christian life, we loudly proclaim, is something which must be lived in this world or nowhere; if we do not serve God in the neighbour we are not serving him.

Some of this reaction is no doubt healthy enough. There can be a false kind of other-worldliness. But are we not reacting a bit too far? Can the centre of all our faith for us mortal men be within these fleeting years? It remains true that the Christian centre of gravity is not in this mortal life at all: and it is from this fact that our threescore years and ten derive their importance and responsibility. It is because we are made for eternity that good government and good neighbour service matter. If the church loses its faith in the future life or soft-pedals it in its public utterance – which it seems now to be too prone to do –

its message is terribly weakened and impoverished. It is failing men at the point of their deepest need and driving them, in default of something better, into jungles of superstition and occultism.

But other-worldliness has another meaning. We speak of the Christian life as a warfare against the world, the flesh and the devil. But in saying it, what do we mean by the world? Or, for that matter, what do we mean by the flesh? (For to think of our physical nature as in itself evil is a profoundly sub-Christian notion and incompatible with the incarnation.) The New Testament writers use the word at least in two senses. On the one hand, 'God so loved the world . . .'; on the other, 'Love not the world nor the things that are in the world, for if any man loves the world, the love of the Father is not in him.' In the first text, world means the human race, the inhabited world (the *oikoumene*), or perhaps the cosmos which God created and loves. In the second, it means human life and society regarded as self-sufficient and self-contained, organized without any regard for God. It means, in other words, what we mean by worldliness. (If anyone speaks of a thoroughly worldly woman, we know what is meant and we recognize the type.) It does not mean just the secular world around us.

Eighteenth-and nineteenth-century evangelicalism shied away from contact with 'the world' – by which it sometimes meant not much more than enjoying what other people enjoyed (theatres, cards, dancing – but not long dinners). The church becomes a world on its own with its 'sacred' art and its 'sacred' music, distinct from – and often far worse than – their secular counterparts.

Here was another false kind of other-worldliness, and against that too we are rightly in reaction. The Christian life is far more than 'religion'. To be interested only in religious matters is certainly no hallmark of a 'real 'Christian; it is rather a symptom of lack of mental vitality or of a narrowness of human sympathy which is far from being a Christian attribute. Christians are not a special kind of men. 'If you prick us, do we not bleed?' We are bound up in a bundle of life with all other men, and we do not inhabit a private Christian hemisphere. To live shut up in a little churchy world is no way to bear witness to Christ as Lord. Our place, surely, is in the common life, sharing the common tasks and interests and opportunities of the human race in God's world, under the lordship of Christ and in responsibility before God. Can we say that the true opposite of worldliness is not other-worldliness but godliness?[1]

All this is now described as involvement, and this is the slogan of 'secular Christianity'. (There is no inherent reason in the nature of things why a modern secular society should not be a Christian society. Secular does not in itself mean secularist.) In a sense, too, this is 'religionless' Christianity. Good and worthwhile secular activities do not require religious authorization; in their own right they are acceptable to God. We need not be always 'dragging religion in.' Nothing is made more Christian or more holy by using pious language about it; that is a matter of quality and motive. The attempt – sometimes urged on us from the pulpit – to make religion cover the whole of life can be merely pietistic and sentimental and can end in the desecration of religion. We ought not to be always thinking about religion. If a surgeon is engaged in meditation while he is removing my appendix my chances of survival will not be high. As William Temple used often to remind us, if we are to do any job to the glory of God (and that means, primarily, to do the job well) our mind must be concentrated on what we are doing.

Christianity covers the whole of life because Christ is the Lord of human life and because the whole world belongs to God. We must see it all in the light of God's will and purpose and glorify him in whatever is true and pure and lovely, in its strength and goodness, not only in its weaknesses. To call God in aid only as a problem-solver or a last resort 'when other helpers fail' is not so far as it ought to be from magic. God is at the centre of all life, secular affairs as well as religious. Religion is one specialized activity through which we retain our faith and our communion with him. And to all the manifold secular activities the religious man brings his own contribution through his own distinctive attitude to life. How much really great art has there been since the West began to abandon its Christian inheritance?

Yet the Christian life is centred in its religion. A literally religionless Christianity would surely be a contradiction in terms. In our new-found zeal for involvement and secularity, are we not at the moment in a certain danger of producing a purely activist Christianity, busy like Martha about many things – whether good works or servicing the machinery – but at the price of forgetting the one thing needful, the inner life and the 'secret discipline'. (Yet what men need today more than anything is some interior quiet and integration.) Christians, we hear it said now, are people who stand for justice and freedom and peace and brotherhood, who must therefore be actively engaged in politics for the changing and Christianizing of society according to God's will revealed in Christ. That is perfectly true, but is it the whole truth? Is it even the most important truth? Surely Christians are primarily people whose lives are 'hid with Christ in God'? A purely activist Christianity is bound in the end, I should say, to become devitalized, if not superficial and indistinguishable from other forms of liberal philanthropic effort – indeed at last from secular humanism. The young men talk as though 'going to church' were unimportant, if not a waste of time which ought to be given to Shelter and Christian Aid. But all these rightful manward activities move outwards from the inner shrine of worship, prayer and communion with God. No horizontal expressions of our faith can be substitutes for the vertical relationship. How can it hope to retain its vitality or resist 'the contagions of the world's slow stain' if it is not constantly nourished and replenished by drawing on the springs of the well of life?

If we are to offer a Christian contribution to the hopes and strivings of the common life, we must have something distinctive to offer – to be in the world, yet somehow not of the world. If the salt, said Jesus, has lost its saltness, it is good for nothing and people throw it out. If the yeast does not retain its yeastiness it will simply be drowned in the dough, in the solid mass of 'worldly' society. Therefore, the more secular it becomes – and this is on the whole, I should say, a right development – the more 'religious', the more supernatural, the more other-worldly must Christianity be. The more active and gregarious we become, the more zealously ought we to safeguard occasions of withdrawal and solitude.

It may be that the really important question now is not whether Christians are too much cut off from the secular world around them, but whether they are too much at home in it. 'Be not shaped to the pattern of this world, but transformed by the renewing of your minds.' What is the mark by which Christians ought to be recognized? Are we perhaps accepting too complacently the values prevalent in our society? For while we ought, I am sure, to be fully 'involved' in it, we ought to be thinking Christianly about it and bringing Christian criticism to bear on it, in the light of our beliefs about God and man. If we take our cue from the world, what shall we have of any importance to say to it which it cannot find out equally well itself?

The churches are now, at last, beginning to realize that we have a social philosophy of our own, but the rank and file membership is not yet aware of it. Unfortunately such protest as it offers is too much confined to sexy shows and pornography. The value of that need not be underrated. Anything that helps to stem the tide of depravity is a contribution towards the good society. But the universal worship of Mammon is surely far more deeply corrupting, perverting our values and poisoning our motives, than the minority cult of Aphrodite. However, just round the corner is a further question – to which, frankly, I do not know the answer. Is there – and if not, ought there to be – anything which markedly differentiates the Christian from other respectable, decent-living citizens? Can there be, or ought there to be, such a thing as a specifically Christian life-style? Such a question may be too easily misunderstood. I am not suggesting that there are jobs or activities which are in themselves more Christian than others. As Dr Munby wrote about this some years ago:

There are no specifically religious concerns ... The religious man is not a man who does one thing rather than another, for example a teacher rather than an industrial manager, or a tennis player rather than a football watcher. There are no concerns more particularly Christian than others.[2]

He had written earlier:

> It is easy to be contemptuous of our modern vulgarities. It is much more difficult for Christians to create a pattern of living in the twentieth century which is neither irrelevant nor escapist.[3]

The church is in the world to change the world, and obviously it is part of the church's mission to help our twentieth-century society, with its complex economic and technical processes, to create a pattern of truly human community in which men can live as God wills men to live. That would be, in some real sense, a Christian life-style. But that is largely a matter of social structuring and appropriate public and political action rather than of personal and private conduct. That is not quite the question that I am raising. What I am asking is whether there is a life-style in the sense of a pattern of private and personal living – in the order of our priorities, for example, possibly even in our domestic budgetting – by which Christians are or should be characterized. If there is, we have lamentably failed to realize it, beyond a few negations like teetotalism – which can only very dubiously be called Christian. Anything would be better than making the Christian life consist in a table of things you mustn't do or of pleasures from which you must abstain. What we want is a positive style of living framed to distinctively Christian scales of value which, both in its creativity and its discipline, both in its width and height and in its depth, would be offering an unspoken criticism not so much of the wickedness of our world as of its aimlessness and its triviality – symptoms of its spiritual poverty. Is such an idea feasible in practice? Many others have tried, without much success, to envisage it. (One obvious difficulty is that life-styles vary with the amount of disposable income.) Would it be possible to extend more widely the idea of Tertiaries under rule – which would clearly have to include the proportions (not the actual amounts) of expenditure on purely personal luxuries and amenities as distinct from the cultural goods of society? It may well be that the rising generation, who are so dissatisfied with the institution, should be encouraged to put their minds to work on this.

110

'Of course you can't go to church,' said a Christian parent, 'once you're grown up. Well, I mean, how can you?' Christianity may or may not be in decline – that is something only God can know. But it is indisputable that the church as an organized institution is. However, the question is, can the world be Christianized without the mission and ministry of the church? We are the first generation of Christians who have had seriously to ask that question. Almost till yesterday it would have sounded gratuitous.

There are, in this country, and still more in Africa, many stirrings of Christian revival which are outside and apparently independent of the framework of institutional Christianity. We have no need to be worrying over that,; we should rather thank God for any new signs of life. The Spirit blows where it listeth. We are not concerned to protect our vested interests, and God is not the monopoly of churchmen. But what ought to be worrying us is this – that so many Christians today regard the church, or what they call 'organized religion', not only as irrelevant and unnecessary to the Christian life but as almost a hindrance to it. And in this they do not seem to be thinking mainly of its scandals, abuses, and corruptions – for whatever its failures, the church is not corrupt – but simply of its being there at all in the form, at least, with which they are familiar.[4] It stands in the way, and we might be better without it. 'The church,' I hear many Christians say, 'is so awful.'

Discounting ignorance and popular prejudice and the muddled thinking endemic in progressivism, what ought to be said positively about this? I do not conceal my fear that at the moment the church, or at any rate the Church of England, of which alone I can speak from inside knowledge, is in danger of failing the people in their need. But let us confine ourselves to the fundamentals. Is it true that 'organized religion' is something which is bound by its very nature to misrepresent what it claims to stand for? Could there be such a thing as churchless Christianity?

There can be pragmatic answers to that question and some

of them we shall in due course consider. But the fundamental answer is theological. The church is an integral part of its own creed: I believe in God, and in Jesus Christ, in the Holy Spirit and in the church. What we have to remember and to insist upon is that the church is the divine society called into being by the act of God and differs in kind from any other society. It is not just a voluntary association like a tennis club or a mutual aid society, which a man decides to join or not to join. There is no question of first becoming a Christian and then deciding whether or not to join it. There is no question of 'joining' it, we *are* it. There can no more be Christians without the church *than* there can be Englishmen without England. The church is prior to the individual and we do not exist as Christians apart from it. Little charismatic groups may spring up, as they are springing up now, spontaneously and label themselves 'No-Church Christianity', asserting that they owe nothing to the church. Yet in fact, had it not been for the church they would never so much as have heard the name of Christ. 'The gospels,' a man may say, 'are enough for me. With them I can be in touch with Christ without all this ecclesiastical apparatus.' But it is the church which gave him the gospels; and the gospels are permeated, as we now know, with the faith of the church in the earliest Christian communities, which they mediate to us in our later age.

There was not first something called Christianity which the church was afterwards organized to propagate. The Christian faith and the church were born together in the decisive experience of Pentecost. God created the church through the resurrection. The Risen Christ lives in the *koinōnia*, which is his body – the organ of his Spirit. The whole Christ, said Augustine, is the Head of the body together with its members. We are not invited graciously to 'join' it, we are incorporated into it. That is what it means to be a Christian. This what we find in the New Testament where – to put it as bluntly, and shockingly, as I can – to be a Christian is to be a churchman, a partaker in the redemptive *koinōnia*. If we want to be scriptural Christians, we are committed to this very 'high' doctrine of the church: which need not mean being 'high-church' in the sense of liking elaborate ceremonial. It is not a matter of Catholic or Protestant. It was John Wesley who said, 'There is no such thing as a solitary Christian.' Or, as Bernard Lord Manning put it: 'All Christian experience is ecclesiastical experience.'

Christian faith and experience are corporate and in their very nature traditional, handed down from one generation to another; for the church is here to transmit what has been given to it in the revelation by which it was constituted, and apart from that it has nothing to offer to anybody. None of us really discovered our Christian faith through our own personal efforts; it was given to us, handed on by those who had received it in their turn from others, and so back and back till we come at last to the original fountain-head. This is true not only about religion but about the elementary human skills, about knowledge, art, literature and music, about the basic principles or morality, even about the right way of playing games. Does not education consist largely in handing on to the next generation the insights and achievements of its predecessors? Without that continuity of tradition no kind of cultural progress would be possible. If every generation had to go back and start all over again at square one, with no common stock of wisdom to draw upon, it would have to run very fast indeed to be able even to stay where it is. The Christian tradition spans the centuries. It brings us a faith which had been lived and tested by men of every race and colour and tongue long before any of us were born or thought of. Into that body of living and growing tradition, succeeding generations have brought their own insights and interpretations, so that Christian faith and experience are cumulative and there is always more to be discovered in it.

No one Christian generation, still less any one individual Christian, can hope to understand or to appropriate the whole wealth in the treasury of the house of God. The Christian faith is the faith of the church as a whole. There will always be 'bits' that we cannot make head or tail of. In saying the creeds we associate ourselves with the faith of the whole church – yet to be completed – trusting that as we share in the life and worship of our own local and particular church, we may grow in understanding and learn more. None of us can live by our own faith alone. We need the support and help of one another. Here, as elsewhere, God's gifts of grace are mediated to us through other people. That does not make them any less the gifts of God.

Thus the Christian church in its nature is a supernatural society – a city of God coming down from heaven – which exists only through the divine initiative. But as the eternal Word was made flesh, so the church, if it is to live in history, must be embodied in organized institutions. These are partly man-made and therefore fallible and conditioned by social and historical forces. Thus the church is 'at one and the same time' both the communion of the saints in light and a human, historical institution like the Inns of Court or the House of Commons. So there will always be strains and tensions between the empirical church and the church 'in heaven'. It is the church which has nurtured the great saints – lights of the world in their several generations. Yet it is composed of sinful men and is therefore always an imperfect witness to the gospel which it exists to proclaim.

There has never been any other church, and on this side of death there never can be. This means that the church is *semper reformanda*, always falling short of the glory of God; but not that the way to make it more Christian is by attempts to dismantle the institution – which is at the moment the radical programme – for that would simply leave Christianity without any external embodiment at all. The question is, would it then be Christianity? Would it be the religion of the Word made flesh? What impact on society could it have? What would be its own chances of survival or of preserving genuine continuity with its original source of inspiration or with the faith of those who have gone before? The idea of a non-institutional Christianity seems to me to be totally unrealistic as well as theologically mistaken.

It is true, no doubt, that at the present moment the sheer weight and complexity of organization threatens to choke the life out of the church. It is, perhaps, a sign of loss of nerve that we go on building more and more machinery, diverting far too much time and energy into secondary, administrative activities at the cost of things that matter a great deal more and which we are primarily here to do. There is need, I am sure, for a drastic simplification and a searching reassessment of our priorities. But the church cannot evade the responsibility of being an organized institution in an increasingly complicated society, or it will become socially irrelevant. Nor can it abdicate from its history. Its traditional forms have been, under God, the structures by which the Christian faith has been sustained and to which we all of us owe our Christianity.

The church does not exist for its own sake. The church is the servant of its mission, which is that of the Lord of the church himself, to set forward God's kingdom in the life of men. That must not be interpreted too moralistically or in a too restrictedly 'religious' way. Politics, industry, science, art and literature are all, potentially, instruments of God's reign, as Christians are at long last beginning to realize; but only too often to conclude that the work of the church is a marginal activity with which Christianity could dispense.

If we want to see a recovery of the church we must give up being weakly apologetic and put beyond all doubt that we do believe in it, not as simply a club for religiously minded people – for the world can carry on perfectly well without that – but as the divinely endowed society and the instrument of Christ's redemptive work. If we want to see a revival of Christianity we must at least make sure that it is presented on the highest level of truth revealed by God, in its mystery and challenge and claim upon us, not cheapened, softened or desupernaturalized.

NOTES

1. Professor Blackham describes the characteristic note of humanism as 'unworldly worldliness, impassioned materialism' (*Objections to Humanism*, Constable, 1964, p. 25). On humanist assumptions it is a little difficult to understand what this unworldliness can mean, beyond unselfishness and devotion to the common good, which many humanists exhibit in ways which put some Christians to shame.

2. Denys Munby, *God and the Rich Society*, Oxford University Press, 1961, p. 178.

3. Ibid., p. 174.

4. Or is 'familiar' the right word? For some of the loudest talk comes from people who know very little about it from inside and are thinking about a conventional image of it.

Index of Names

Abelard, Peter   61, 102
Anselm   39
Archimedes   30, 32
Aristotle   38, 43, 67
Arnold, M.   31, 103
Auden, W. H.   11
Augustine   50, 88, 112

Baelz, P.   60, 61, 62
Barth, K.   50, 51
Berger, P.   6, 11, 33, 61
Bernard of Cluny   61
Blackham, H. J.   115
Blake, W.   18, 95
Bonhoeffer, D.   51
Braithwaite, R. B.   100
Bronowski, J.   61
Butler, J.   48, 88
Butt, R.   103

Camus, A.   10
Clark, Lord   1, 9, 11, 62
Claudius Lysias   68

Dante   57
David   59
Descartes, R.   41

Dodd, C. H.   15, 94
Dodds, E. R.   11
Dunstan, G. R.   103

Edward the Confessor   77
Edwards, D. L.   103
Einstein, A.   31

Farrer, A. M.   15, 61f.
Fletcher, J.   100
Freud, S.   14, 70

Gummer, J. S.   104

Hailsham, Lord   86
Hamlet   54
Hare, R. M.   103
Héloïse   102
Herodotus   81
Hick, J.   39f., 47, 60, 61
Hodgson, L.   47
Homer   57
Hooker, R.   88
Hügel, Baron von   7
Hume, D.   31, 38

James, St   61

Jefferson, T. 67
Jenkins, D. E. 9, 11
Job 13
John, St 32, 54
John Scotus Erigena 50

Kant, I. 38, 71, 75, 79, 84, 102
Knight, Mrs. M. 88
Knox, J. 29

Lang, C. G. 55
Locke, J. 67
Lucretius 40

MacIntyre, A. 61
Manning, B. L. 112f.
Martha 108
Martin, H. vii
Marx, K. 70, 81
Mary the Virgin 53, 59
Michelangelo 55
Mill, J. S. 66
Milton, J. 57, 72, 83, 103
Montefiore, H. 29
Moses 14, 45, 95
Moule, C. F. D. 19, 29
Munby, D. 109f., 116
Murdoch, I. 76, 83, 103

Newton, I. 31
Niebuhr, R. 25
Nietzsche, F. 19, 65

Origen 59

Paley, W. 39
Pannenberg, W. 61, 103

Pascal, B. 45
Paton, H. J. 41, 61
Paul, St 4, 32, 61, 67, 75, 88, 96
Peacocke, A. R. 11, 29
Plato 38, 49, 73, 82, 95

Ramsey, I. T. 62, 103
Ramsey, P. 101, 104
Robinson, J. A. T. 29, 100
Root, H. x
Roubiczek, P. 103
Russell, B. 40
Ryle, G. 27f., 72, 74, 103

Santucci, L. 8, 29
Shakespeare, W. 73
Shaw, G. B. 67
Shelley, P. B. 53
Smith, P. Nowell 103
Socrates 95
Storr, A. 58, 62

Temple, W. ix, 32, 64, 107
Thomas Aquinas 33, 39, 88
Thomas, G. F. 104
Titian 55

Vidler, A. R. x
Virgil 57

Wesley, J. 112
Wilson, Bryan 11
Winter, G. 90, 103
Woods, G. F. 103

Zahrnt, H. 29